KINGDOM TREASURY
VOLUME ONE

UNLEASHING THE POWER OF ANCIENT TZEDAKAH MYSTERIES

"... Therefore every scribe instructed concerning the Kingdom of Heaven is like a householder who brings out of his treasure things new and old." – Matthew 13:52

Anderick Biddle

Copyright © 2012 by Anderick Biddle

KINGDOM TREASURY VOLUME ONE – UNLEASHING THE POWER OF ANCIENT TZEDAKAH MYSTERIES
by Anderick Biddle
Printed in the United States of America

ISBN-13: 978-0615748191

All rights reserved solely by the author. The author guarantees all contents are original and do not infringe upon the legal rights of any other person or work. No part of this book may be reproduced in any form without the permission of the author. The views expressed in this book are not necessarily those of the publisher.

Unless otherwise indicated, Bible quotations are taken from the New King James Version of the Bible.

DEDICATION

This book is dedicated to all of the people whose demonstrations of generosity and kindness towards myself and others have inspired me.

SPECIAL THANKS

I would like to thank my editor Janet Spiewak, you are truly a gift from God.

Thank you to my good friend Marnelle Billups and Web Man Graphics, whose expertise are responsible for this book cover.

Thank you to my wife Shirron, whose love, patience, encouragement and faith in me has helped make this work possible.

CONTENTS

INTRODUCTION..5
Chapter 1: COMING OUT OF THE TOWER OF BABEL................ 17
Chapter 2: FOLLOWING FATHER ABRAHAM............................... 23
Chapter 3: THE OBJECTIVE OF SCRIPTURE................................ 30
Chapter 4: DEFINING REAL KINGDOM LOVE............................. 42
Chapter 5: DO YOU KNOW THE HEAVENLY FATHER?................ 52
Chapter 6: WHY THE LORD KNOWS THE RIGHTEOUS............... 62
Chapter 7: ABRAHAM'S TZEDAKAH... 71
Chapter 8: ABRAHAM'S PRAYER FOR TZEDAKAH..................... 80
Chapter 9: BECOMING A TREE OF TZEDAKAH.......................... 92
Chapter 10: SEEKING TZEDAKAH AT ALL TIMES....................... 105
Chapter 11: INCREASING YOUR NOBILITY AND EQUITY
IN THE KINGDOM.. 111
Chapter 12: THE MINISTRY OF MESSIAH................................... 119
Chapter 13: SONS OF THE KINGDOM.. 128
Chapter 14: HOW TO CARRY YOUR CROSS............................... 137
Chapter 15: THE PURPOSE OF THE GOSPEL.............................. 151
Chapter 16: THE MASTER KEY TO THE KINGDOM..................... 156
PERSONAL TZEDAKAH ACTION PLAN...................................... 166

INTRODUCTION
KINGDOM LEARNING

"Be diligent to present yourself approved to God, a worker who does not need to be ashamed, rightly dividing the word of truth."
2Timothy 2:15

Millions of people in our world today are working diligently to acquire the approval of the people around them. Even in ministry there are believers who are careful to make sure they have the approval of their denomination, peers or family. Often times giving in to this pressure to conform and seek out man's approval causes an individual to miss their call to learning and living at a higher level, or it may cost them the chance to live out their dreams. This book was not born out of conformity and seeking the approval of men. As a matter of fact, it has mostly been the opposite. This particular book and series is a product of my desire to be diligent to show myself approved to God.

    The King James translation of 2 Timothy 2:15 is that we are to "study to show ourselves approved unto God". This is the key to our understanding of what we must do to acquire God's approval. We must **STUDY**. The word and idea of studying conveys being fully engaged or immersed in what one desires to learn. This means the best and most effective way to learn something is to be fully engrossed within the context and culture of what you want to learn.

    For example, it would not make sense to us that a child who wants to become a professional basketball player should go to a football field and learn about basketball from football coaches and football players. No, we would tell that child to go and immerse himself as much as possible in a basketball culture and environment.

But why am I saying this? Because although the holy Scriptures in the Old Testament we diligently study have been translated into various languages, the original writers were ALL Hebrew people, who communicated through Hebrew language, within the context of a Hebrew culture. As a result, I believe the language and culture in which we can gain the fullest meaning and understanding of the Old Testament Scriptures is the Hebrew language and culture. Without this particular perspective and preconception, we are lost in translation. Also for this reason I choose to use the Messiah's Hebrew name YESHUA (יהושיע) instead of the most often used translation of Jesus. Which by the way would also be better translated Joshua (יהושיע), rather than Jesus. Obviously, this topic in itself needs further discussion, which we will not take time for in this work. However, I feel it is important that you understand at least the idea behind preferring to use the more accurate name of our Messiah.

     When I say that this book was not born out of conformity to the approval of peers and denominational ideologies, this is what I mean. In writing this book, I did not set the limits and boundaries based on traditional or contemporary context and meaning. Instead, as much as possible, I sought to try and understand these ancient writings of Old Testament scripture through the lens of the ancient culture and language in which it was written.

For that reason I also thought it appropriate to utilize Hebrew methods and principles of study and discipleship, which are used to uncover deeper truths and treasures of wisdom from the Scriptures.

One of the methods I followed to interpret the Scriptures are the seven principles for biblical interpretation developed by Rabbi Hillel, which are shown on the following chart.

Principle 1
- Kal vechomer- "light and heavy"
- The argument from a minor premise to a major one

Principle 2
- Gezerah shavah "cut equally"
- Teaching based upon an analogy or reference from one verse to another

Principle 3
- Binyan av mikatuv echad "building a teaching principle based on one verse" Main proposition is derived from one verse

Principle 4
- Binyan aav mishnai katuvim "building a teaching principle based on two verses
- Main proposition is derived from two verses

Principle 5
- Kelal uferat-perat vekelal "general and specific- specific and general
- Teaching from a general principle to a specific one, or from a specific principle to a general one

Principle 6
- Keyotza bo bamakom acher "As comes from it in another place
- Teaching based upon what is similar in another passage

Principle 7
- Devar halamed meinyano "A word that is learned from its own issue"
- A matter that is learned from its own subject

Before I explain the second method of study used in developing this book, let me first show you the significance of the Hebrew language itself. Take a look at the following chart of Hebrew letters, numbers and their symbolic meanings.

NAME	BOOK	NUMBER	SOUND	LITERAL MEANING	SYMBOLIC MEANING
Aleph	א	1	silent	ox, bull	strength,
Bet/Vet	ב	2	b/v	tent, house	household, in
Gimmel	ג	3	g	camel	pride, lift up
Dalet	ד	4	d	door	pathway/enter
Hey	ה	5	h	window	behold, reveal
Vav	ו	6	v	nail	and, hook, secure
Zayin	ז	7	z	weapon	cut, cut off
CHet	ח	8	CH	fence, hedge	private, separate
Tet	ט	9	t	twist, a snake	to surround
Yud	י	10	y	hand	work, to make
Kaf/Chaf	כ	20	k	palm of hand	open/ to allow
Lamed	ל	30	L	staff/goad	control/ toward
Mem	מ	40	m	water	chaos, massive
Nun	נ	50	n	fish/seed	activity, live
Samech	ס	60	s	hand of staff	support
Ayin	ע	70	silent	eye	see, experience
Pe/Fe	פ	80	p/ph	mouth	speak, word
Tzadi	צ	90	tz/ts	laying on side	to hunt, desire
Qof	ק	100	q	back of head	behind, the least
Resh	ר	200	r	head	person, highest
Sin/Shin	ש	300	s/sh	teeth	consume, destroy
Tav/Tau	ת	400	t	sign, cross	sign, covenant

As you examine this chart, you will see that each letter of the Hebrew alphabet has a numerical value. This means that each Hebrew word also has a numerical value. For example, the Hebrew word for father is *"Ab"* (אב), and as you can see it is formed from the letters *aleph* (א), which has a numerical value of 1 and *beit*, (ב) which has a numerical value of 2. Combined, these form the word *"Ab"* which has a numerical value of 3, the sum of 1+2.

    Furthermore, you can also see that each letter of the Hebrew alphabet is also a picture of some sort and has symbolic meaning. This means that each Hebrew word is also a picture or image and can not only be defined by words, but can be illustrated through its pictorial meaning. For instance, in Hebrew you can not only define the word for father, but you can actually see a picture or illustration of what a father does. As you read this book, you will see the pictorial illustration of the Hebrew word father and a variety of other interesting word pictures.

    The Hebrew name for studying and investigating Scriptures in this manner is called *"midrash"* and is also one of the methods of study employed throughout this book. *Midrash* is founded on the idea that not only every word in the Scriptures has meaning, but that every single letter of Scripture should be examined in order to comprehend Scripture in the most meaningful way. According to the *midrash*, the Scriptures can also be studied on four different and successive levels. These are shown in the following chart.

Sod- mystery, revelation

Derash- application, homiletical commentary

Remez- hint, or allegorical explanation

Peshat- simple, or literal interpretation

The first level of studying Scripture is called the *"peshat"*, which is simple, literal interpretation or surface meaning of a Scripture. For example, when the Scriptures says the Jesus wept, we understand that He was literally moved to tears (John 11:35). The second level of study is called *"Remez,"* which refers to the hint or allegorical understanding. The *remez* level of studying Scripture is the foundation of the parables and allegorical teachings. Simply put a *remez* can be identified in Scripture through examining repetitions, the mention of names, numbers, dates and other things that appear to be peculiar. One example of a *remez* is when the Scripture says the Jesus appointed 70 others to go before Him into every city He was about to go to in pairs of two (Luke 10:1). What is this hinting or alluding towards? Just as the LORD through Moses appointed 70 elders to bear witness to the teachings and instructions of God and to judge the people accordingly, Yeshua was also appointing 70 to bear witness to the teachings and instructions of God and to judge accordingly (Numbers 11:16-17, 24-25).

The third level of *midrash* is the *"derash,"* which again refers to the direct application or meaning of the Scripture. This is a very important part of study, because it ensures we understand what we are to do with the knowledge of Scripture. In other words, the d*erash*, ensures that we are doers of the Word and not hearers only. The fourth and final level of *midrash* is *"sod"* and refers to the mysteries or secrets of the Kingdom that come directly from the Spirit. The *sod* is not knowledge that is secret because it has been kept from certain individuals, but it is a higher level of knowledge or wisdom that is too infinite to be contained and fully explained through words. It is a wisdom that comes directly from the Spirit realm and cannot be accurately communicated through words. For example, when an angel revealed the wisdom of God's plan to Daniel, he became overwhelmed and was unable to fully communicate what had been revealed through words (Daniel 10:14-16).

During His teaching on the parable of the sower, Yeshua told His disciples that it was given to them to know the mysteries of the Kingdom of God (Mark 4:11). One example of *sod* being revealed in Scripture is when Yeshua tells Peter that He did not come to know that He was the Christ, from flesh and blood, but by revelation of the Spirit of God (Matthew 16:17).

According to the *midrash,* something incredible happens when a person comes to understand the Scriptures on all four levels. Interestingly, if you take the first letters of P̱eshat, R̲emez, D̲erash and S̲od you are left with the letters PRDS, which in Hebrew is written (from right to left) as follows (פרדס) and is pronounced *"pardes"*, which means paradise. In other words, the idea is that when one fully understands a Scripture from peshat to sod it brings forth a greater manifestation of the Kingdom of Heaven on Earth.

Be a Doer of the Word

"But be doers of the Word, and not hearers only, deceiving yourselves… But he who looks into the perfect law of liberty and continues in it, he is not a forgetful hearer, but a doer of the work. This one will be blessed in what he does." **James 1:22, 25**

In Hebrew, "disciple" is the word *"talmid"* and is one who learns to walk according to the Torah (teachings and instructions of God), by literally following and imitating the life and character of a rabbi (or teacher). Contrary to many schools and even churches today, a disciple's learning was not complete by hearing, studying and memorizing Scripture. Rather, a disciple's learning or knowledge was complete only by doing and experiencing. This is why Yeshua and His brother, James, both explained that an individual is not blessed just because they hear (and learn) the instructions of God, but only because they "follow" or carry out the instructions. (Matthew 6:24-28; James 1:22-25).

Unfortunately, many believers today act as if the goal of discipleship is to increase one's good knowledge. It is not! As a matter of fact, the goal of hearing the Scriptures is not even to increase your faith. Faith is a byproduct of hearing the word of God (Romans 10:17). In fact, the goal of hearing and learning the Word of God is to increase one's good "WORKS". It is not how much you know that matters; it is how much you do.

Potential vs. Kinetic Energy

While many people are content with only having the scriptural knowledge of the Kingdom of Heaven, knowledge in and of itself is only *potential* energy, and the problem with potential energy lies in its definition. That is, potential energy is <u>unrealized</u> capability. Or to put it simply, it does not cause any real difference nor does it change reality. Acting upon knowledge is *kinetic* energy which accomplishes work and changes reality. Yeshua is interested in changing the reality of Earth into the reality of the Kingdom of Heaven (Matthew 6:10).

      This again is why James states that only the "doer of <u>the work</u> is blessed in whatever he does" (James 1:25). Take another look at the Sermon on the Mount, you'll notice that Yeshua did not say, let your light shine by letting the world hear how much you know. No, instead He said, *"Let your light so shine before men, that they may see your good works and glorify your Father in heaven."* (Matthew 5:16). Your family, community and the world, needs to "SEE" you "<u>DOING</u>" good things, not hear about you learning good things. With this in mind we would probably be much better off thinking of a disciple of Yeshua as an apprentice, one who is learning to do work. While a student is one who is only learning, an apprentice is one who gets on the job training. An apprentice does not wait until they are done gaining knowledge before they get to work, they are already working. On that note, that means we need leaders in the family, the Church, government and business who not only teach, but train the next generation how to function.

Follow the Leader

"...how God anointed Jesus of Nazareth with the Holy Spirit and with power, who went about doing good and healing all who were oppressed by the devil, for God was with Him." **Acts 10:38**

As we mentioned earlier the purpose of the Torah or God's divine teaching and instruction is to provoke divine actions or good works. Since Yeshua came to show us how to fulfill the Torah, we can either spend years learning to become a master scholar with the correct interpretation of the Torah, or we can just take a look at the works of Yeshua and then emulate Him. This was the beauty and simplicity of following a rabbi. The idea was that all you had to do to fulfill the Torah, was do what they did, say what they said and act as they acted. This is truly the method in which children learn best. They emulate their parents, which doesn't mean just to imitate, but to strive be equal to or even surpass. Even Yeshua proclaimed to emulate the Father:

"...Most assuredly, I say to you, the Son can do nothing of Himself, but what He sees the Father do. For whatever He does, the Son does in like manner." **John 5:19**

While some prefer the "do as I say and not as I do" method of teaching, anyone who has children knows this does not work. Why? Because people are programmed to duplicate the examples they see. So, here are a few important questions we must ask... "What are we looking at? Who are we looking at? And what do we see them doing?" What does a child see their mother or father doing? What does the citizen see their political leaders doing? What does the church see their pastors or ministers doing? Because they and you are learning whatever you or they are seeing and doing.

The efficiency and effectiveness of Yeshua's teaching was that He did not have to speak with His mouth in order to teach His followers. He understood that actions indeed speak louder than words. Here are a few more questions for us to answer: If you are a parent, what would your children learn from you, if you could not speak and they could only observe your actions? If you are a pastor or minister, what would your followers learn from you if you could not speak and they could only observe your actions and behaviors? Well, whatever they would learn then, is what they are learning from you now.

Did We Misunderstand the Mandate?

Maybe we have misinterpreted the Great Commission. Perhaps that's the reason it appears the Church is trying to make disciples of Yeshua (Jesus) mostly by *talking* about Yeshua. But not even Yeshua (Jesus) made disciples by talking about Himself and what He would do. As a matter of fact, many didn't really understand who He was. Even when they came to arrest Him, they only knew him because Judas signaled them with a kiss (Matthew 16:13-14; 26:48-49). So what does the Great Commission actually instruct us to do? How does it instruct us to make disciples? Well, in case you don't remember it or have not analyzed it in a while, here it is.

*"Go therefore and make disciples of all nations, baptizing them in the name of the Father and of the Son and of the Holy Spirit, teaching them to **"OBSERVE"** all the things that I have commanded*

you; and lo I am with you always; even to the end of the age. Amen" **Matthew 28:19-20** (emphasis added)

WOW! There it is! Yeshua did not command His followers to make followers by primarily through lectures and sermons. No, He commanded His followers to make followers by giving them something to **OBSERVE** and to follow (John 13:15).

So what is the church learning today? That question can be answered by observing what the church is presently doing. Furthermore, you can even predict what the next generation of "Christians" will do by what they are now observing.

CHAPTER 1
COMING OUT OF THE TOWER OF BABEL

"And I heard another voice from heaven saying, come out of her, my people lest you share in her sins, and lest you receive of her plagues." **Revelation 18:4**

This scripture is one that really intrigued me for many years as I studied the Word of God. It's found in the book of Revelation where the fall of Babylon is foretold. If you are or have been a serious student of the Scriptures at some time in your life, then you probably know that Babylon has historically been an enemy of God's people. What intrigues me is not the final fall of Babylon, but rather that God is still calling for His people to come out of Babylon. There are many questions that come to mind in light of this scripture. What are God's people doing in Babylon? What is Babylon? And where is it?

In order to answer these questions and better understand the significance of Babel, let's go back and examine the first mention or introduction to Babel. I believe that is where we will better understand this mysterious place where many of God's people are, but may not even know it. Of course, I'm not talking about God's people being geographically located in Babel, but spiritually. Let's read and examine the first introduction to Babel.

"Now the whole earth had one language and one speech. And it came to pass, as they journeyed from the east, that they found a plain in the land of Shinar, and they dwelt there. Then they said to

one another, come let us make bricks and bake them thoroughly. They had brick for stone and they had asphalt for mortar. And they said, come let us build ourselves a city and a tower whose top is in the heavens; let us make a name for ourselves, lest we be scattered abroad over the face of the whole earth. But the LORD came down to see the city and the tower which the sons of men had built, and the LORD said, indeed the people are one and they all have one language, and this is what they begin to do; now nothing that they propose to do will be withheld from them. Come let us go down and there confuse their language, that they may not understand one another's speech. So the LORD scattered them abroad from there over the face of all the earth, and they ceased building the city. Therefore its name is Babel, because there the LORD confused the language of all the earth; and from there the LORD scattered them abroad over the face of all the earth." **Genesis 11:1-9**

It is interesting to note that modern archeologist have determined that the location of the tower of Babel, which also later became the center of the Babylonian empire was in the area we now call Iraq. It was in this region where the whole world, speaking the same language, came together to build a "tower" whose top reached heaven. However, this wasn't just some extremely tall sky scraper that they want to build. By just reading on the surface without getting deeper teaching, you might get the impression that God is against sky scrapers.

What is this tower they were trying to build? Let me warn you that this is about to get pretty interesting. What I am about to show you may even be a bit shocking for some, but here we go. The Hebrew word translated as tower here is the word *"migdal,"* and it means tower in the sense of something that is high, but it also means… **"a pulpit."** Yes, you read that right. This is the same name as the piece of furniture that a minister stands behind to preach the Word of God.

In this context, if you replace the word "tower" with "pulpit," it would read that they came together to build a pulpit that reached Heaven. Hmmm? Now at this point, I'm sure this may sound strange, because it sounds like what they are trying to build is a ministry which reaches the Heavens. If this was the case, then why would God be against it? Surely God would not be against a ministry that wants to reach Heaven, or would He?

Let's break the suspense. The problem that God had with the "pulpit" of Babel, is that the goal or mission of it was to reach Heaven and not Earth. Furthermore, the word *migdal* is also a picture of something that is fortified or walled off from the surrounding community. In this context, the Tower of Babel is a picture of a ministry (or pulpit) that is walled off from the people or community and is only interested in reaching Heaven, not the community. Their goal was to minister to God and not minister to the *needs of the people of God*.

What is interesting is the name God gives the place after He condemns the type of ministry (or pulpit) they were trying to build. He calls it "Babel." A word that means "confusion." It's where we get the word "babbling."

In other words, the pulpit of Babel is a picture of a ministry that was all talk and no action. Its goal was to build a pulpit or tower that reached the Heavens. This idea is completely contrary to the ideals of the Kingdom of God, which is not to build pulpits and buildings, but to build people and communities. So now when we read Revelation 18, we can see that God is not calling His people to come out of physical Babylon, but to come out of the ministries where the focus is not on reaching the community and building the people. God wants us to understand that the way to reach Heaven is by reaching people.

In opposition to Babel, we see in Exodus when God's people are told to build a tabernacle and a place where God's presence can dwell among them, they are instructed to build a tent, or dwelling place for God out of animals' hides that had been sacrificed so that the poor and needy among them would have food. Quite a contrast between the idea of building the Kingdom called Babylon vs. building the Kingdom of Heaven. Babylon is built on babbling, it is all talk and very little action. On the contrary the Kingdom of God is built through actions and laboring in love for others. Babylon builds buildings, while the Kingdom of God builds people.

COVER YOUR MOUTH

"Be silent, all flesh, before the LORD, for He is aroused from His holy habitation!" **Zechariah 2:13**

So what do we do? How do we make sure that we are not just babbling and neglecting to produce real Kingdom fruit? Well, if you are concerned that you not be identified with religious babblers, one thing you can do is to simply cover your mouth. Interestingly, the Hebrew word for covering one's mouth is **"tsome"**, and it also means *to fast*. Through the prophet Isaiah, God gives us a very clear picture and understanding of why He wants us to fast or cover our mouths. Furthermore, He also explains the goal or purpose of fasting. Take a look:

"Is this not the fast that I have chosen: To loose the bonds of wickedness, to undo the heavy burdens, to let the oppressed go free, and that you break every yoke? Is it not to share your bread with

the hungry, and that you bring to your house the poor who are cast out; when you see the naked, that you cover him, and not hide yourself from your own flesh? Then your light shall break forth like the morning, your healing shall spring forth speedily, and your righteousness shall go before you; The glory of the LORD shall be your rear guard. Then you shall call, and the LORD will answer; You shall cry, and He will say Here I am. If you take away the yoke from your midst, the pointing of the finger, and speaking wickedness, if you extend your soul to the hungry and satisfy the afflicted soul, then you light shall dawn in the darkness, and your darkness shall be as the noonday. The LORD will guide you continually, and satisfy your soul in drought, and strengthen your bones; You shall be like a watered garden, and like a spring of water, whose waters do not fail. Those from among you shall build the old waste places; you shall raise up the foundations of many generations; and you shall be called the Repairer of the Breach, the Restorer of Streets to dwell in."
Isaiah 58:6-12

In this passage, we see that the purpose of fasting or covering ones mouth is not just to abstain from food as an end in itself. Neither is the purpose of fasting that God would be moved to sympathize with your hunger, but that *you* would sympathize with *someone else's hunger or lack!* It is a time where you sacrifice something (namely food and water) and go without, so that someone else doesn't have to go without. It is a time to clothe the naked and help the homeless. In essence, fasting is about covering your mouth and focusing on helping others through acts of righteousness. It is about personally sacrificing in order to restore, repair and rebuild a foundation for many generations. It is about building the local community of the Kingdom of God on a foundation of righteousness.

Not coincidentally, it is after God scatters the worshipers at the pulpit of Babel, that we are introduced to our father Abraham, who God calls out of the land of Ur of the Chaldeans, which was in the area of Babylon. If the spirit of Babel is to try to reach Heaven through babbling worship and building religious buildings, then the spirit of Abraham is to reach people and build communities who need Heaven to come to Earth. Abraham is not only the father of our faith, but his life and ministry are the example that the children and seed of Abraham should follow. As you continue reading, you will discover treasures of wisdom from the life of our father Abraham and his seed, that will transform your thinking.

Chapter 1 Power Points

- The Tower of Babel is a church or religious community that does not reach out to help people or the local community. It is an institution that focuses more on hearing the word than doing the good works we are instructed to do by the word.
- The solution to Babel or babbling is to prioritize good works over good words.
- While Babylon focuses on building religious buildings and institutions, the true mindset of the Kingdom and the seed of Abraham is to build people and communities.

CHAPTER 2

FOLLOWING FATHER ABRAHAM

"Jesus answered them, I told you and you do not believe. The works that I do in My Father's name, they bear witness of Me... If I do not do the works of My Father, do not believe Me; but if I do, though you do not believe Me, believe the works, that you may know and believe that the Father is in Me and I in Him." **John 10: 25, 37-38**

This scripture is one that has deeply impacted me, changed my perspective and understanding of why anyone should be inclined to believe the gospel. In essence, Yeshua is saying that it is not what He says or preaches that validates who He is, but rather the work He is doing. Incredibly, He is saying, although He is the Son of God, don't just believe His words, but believe because of His works! It was not His sermons or His teachings that was final evidence that He was from the Father, but the fact that He *did* the works of His Father. So here are several questions for the believers to answer.

1. If Yeshua (Jesus) the Son of God, did not expect people to believe on Him and follow Him based on His words (or preaching and teaching) alone, should you?
2. If Yeshua explained that people should believe Him because He did the works of the Father, then should they believe you because of your words?
3. If doing the works of the Father validates the Gospel, then should you also being doing the works of the Father?
4. And lastly, what are the works of the Father?

I'll let you answer the first three questions on your own and take as much time as you need to answer them...

Okay, now that you're done, in the next section we are going to discuss the works of the Father. If you profess to be a "follower" of Yeshua and Yeshua followed the Father then we need to make sure we know what the works of the Father are.

THE WORKS OF THE FATHER

"For the Father loves the Son, and shows Him all things that He Himself does..." **John 5:20**

Thank our Heavenly Father for this scripture and the fact that the Father *will* show His children what He does, because He loves them...

Not only does this Scripture teach us that God will show His children the work He does, but it actually goes on to explain that He will show us how to do even greater works. Wow! Isn't that just characteristic of a loving parent? They want their children to do and accomplish more than they have. Now of course when He speaks of greater works, He isn't talking about exceeding Him in quality, but quantity. And if that doesn't quite make sense yet, don't worry I'll bring more clarity to that idea shortly.

We can begin to understand what the works of the Father are by defining and understanding the word or title "Father." In biblical Hebraic culture a person's name was not just some arrangement of letters whose only purpose or use was in speaking to or about an individual, but a name was also a title. Therefore, a name is a description of a person's character, their profession, their position and their possessions (or what they are entitled to). A person's name or title could also reveal their profession or their work. However, this is not a concept exclusive to biblical history.

Many last names of people today are indicators of what their ancestors did. The following are examples of last names that indicate the line of work done by their ancestors: The last name Smith, indicates someone whose craft was metalwork or blacksmith. The name Taylor, indicates someone whose craft was working as a tailor. And the last name Fisher, indicates someone whose line of work was fishing. Obviously we could go on listing the meaning and significance of many more names, but for the sake of time let us continue.

WHO OR WHAT IS A FATHER?

What does the name "father" mean? In Hebrew the word for father is "*ab*" (or *abba* for dear father or daddy). However, when we define a word in Hebrew, we usually get more meaning, because every Hebrew letter is also a number, as well as a picture of something. This means that we can not only define a Hebrew word, but we can also understand it by its pictorial image. So, since I'm pretty sure we all know the definition of father in the parental sense of the word, let's focus on the pictograph. The word "*ab*" is formed from two Hebrew letters "*alef*", which is a picture of an ox and represents strength and the letter "*beit*" (or "*bet*"), which is a picture of a tent and represents house or household. When you combine these two letters, the word "*ab*" is the strength of the tent, which is a picture of a tent-pole. This means that **a father is one who raises up or holds up a household**. In other words, a father sustains a house and keeps it standing, which makes him the strength of the house.

This means that if someone is to do the work of "*ab*" (or "*abba*"), their line of work is sustaining people and households. Just as the function of a tent-pole is to lift the tent off the ground and out of the dirt, the function or role of the father is to lift people up from lowly places and fathers are the reason that a number of individuals are still standing. To confirm this, let's take a look at Yeshua's description of the Father's work of raising up those who are at their lowest and most humble.

> "But Jesus answered them, My Father has been working until now, and I have been working…For as the Father raises the dead and gives life to them, even so the Son gives life to whom He will." **John 5:17, 21**

Scripture records that Yeshua literally raised three people from the dead, so this Scripture is speaking figuratively, as well as literally. Obviously, we know who the literal dead are, those who have no more breath in their bodies. But who are the figuratively dead spoken of here? The (metaphorically) dead are those living far beneath their potential. They are the ones buried under the burdens of life, separated from vital resources. The "dead" have been broken by life: mentally, emotionally, physically or spiritually. These are the ones to whom the Father seeks to give life.
 As a matter of fact, the word translated here in the Greek as "gives life," is a word that means to "revitalize," to endow with life, or to make more spirited/energetic. These are individuals whose vitality or batteries have run out or run low and need to be re-energized and given a boost. Some need a boost emotionally, some physically, some mentally, some economically and some spiritually.

THE FUNCTION OF THE FATHER

Now, in order to legitimately establish something as a biblical doctrine there must be at least two or three "witnesses" of the same concept (Deuteronomy 19:15). So are there other Scriptures that speak of the (work of) God our Heavenly Father raising up the lowly or humble? Of course, here are a few:

"Surely He scorns the scornful, but gives grace to the humble."
Proverbs 3:34
"... God resists the proud, but gives grace to the humble." **1 Peter 5:5**
"Therefore humble yourselves under the mighty hand of God, that He may exalt you in due time," **1 Peter 5:6**
"God resists the proud, but gives grace to the humble." **James 4:6**
"Humble yourselves in the sight of the LORD and He will lift you up."
James 4:10
"Fear not, for I am with you; Be not dismayed, for I am your God. I will strengthen you, yes I will help you, I will uphold you with My righteous right hand." **Isaiah 41:10**

Out of all of the Scriptures above, if I could only choose one to make to point that God our Father seeks to lift up, hold up and sustain weakened persons, I would use Isaiah 41:10. The Hebrew word used in this verse for uphold, is the word *"tamak,"* to help, follow close, to hold up and to sustain.

In order to clarify how God raises up individuals from lowly places the same way a tent pole raises up a tent from the ground, let's examine the concepts of humility and grace. The word used in Proverbs 3:34 for humble is the Hebrew word *"anav,"* meaning depressed, afflicted, hurt, weak, needy or poor. The Hebrew word used for grace is *"chen,"* meaning to favor and give a grant of something in order to empower. To put it simply, God gives *grace* to the *humble* = God *empowers* the *needy*. **God's grace is a grant from the treasury and resources of Heaven to assist and empower the**

needy. That also means when someone asks God for His grace on behalf of someone or some cause, they are not only acting as an intercessor, but as a grant writer.

This is the essence of the gospel of the Kingdom! That the Eternal King has granted the lowly and needy access to the resources and abundant living of His Kingdom. Look how the apostle Paul described his ministry:

"But none of these things move me, nor do I count my life dear to myself, so that I may finish my race with joy, and the ministry which I received from the Lord Jesus, to testify to the Gospel of the grace of God." **Acts 20:24**

Elevate and Empower

So the focus of the gospel is to elevate the depressed, oppressed, lowly, needy and poor to the level and heights of the Kingdom of Heaven. This is the work of the Father and of the Messiah Yeshua, to strengthen and elevate the weak and the poor and the needy. Take a look at how the following Scriptures describe the work of God.

"Who is like the LORD our God...He raises the poor out of the dust, and lifts the needy out the ash heap, that He may seat him with princes – with the princes of His people. He grants the barren woman a home, like a joyful mother of children." **Psalm 113:5, 7-9**

"For the word of the LORD is right, and all His work is done in truth. He loves righteousness and justice: The Earth is full of the goodness of the LORD." **Psalm 33:4-5**

"Come and see the works of God: He is awesome in His doing toward the sons of men."
Psalm 66:5

"By awesome deeds in righteousness, You will answer us, O God of our salvation."
Psalm 65:5a

"The works of the LORD are great, studied by all who have pleasure in them. His work is honorable and glorious; and His righteousness endures forever. He has made His wonderful works to be remembered; The LORD is gracious and full of compassion. He has given food to those who fear Him; He will ever be mindful of His covenant" **Psalm 111: 2-7**

"I will meditate on the glorious splendor of Your majesty, And on Your wondrous works. Men shall speak of the might of Your awesome acts, and I will declare Your greatness. They shall utter the memory of Your great goodness and shall sing of Your righteousness. The LORD is gracious and full of compassion, slow to anger and great in mercy. The LORD is good to all, and His tender mercies are over all His works." **Psalm 145:5-10**

Chapter 2 Power Points:

- Our works not our words are the truest witness of who we are and what we believe.
- Doing the works of the Father is the evidence that the Father is in you. Even Yeshua's ministry was validated by His works and not His words.
- The works of the Father are to uphold and help sustain others in need.

CHAPTER 3

THE OBJECTIVE OF Scripture

There is a very peculiar Hebrew word that is used to describe God's works of kindness and generosity towards the children of men. As a matter of fact, this word and concept is spoken of in Scripture *more than faith, heaven and hell combined!* The sheer number of times that the Scripture speaks of this word/concept is so overwhelming that it is obviously the primary objective of Scripture. So what is the word that describes God's goodness and generosity and is the primary objective of Scripture?

"TZEDAKAH"

"I have proclaimed the good news of the righteous in the great assembly;" **Psalms 40:9**

Tzedakah, pronounced *"tsuh-dah-kah,"* or *"tsuh-dee-kah"* is a word that is usually translated into the English language as righteousness, but is often times translated as justice. It was this idea of t*zedakah* that Yeshua had in mind when He proclaimed that we must "seek first the Kingdom of God and His *righteousness*" or *tzedekah* (Matthew 6:33, emphasis added).

As a matter of fact, Yeshua, thought so highly of this idea of righteousness or *tzedakah* that He taught that we should focus more on seeking God's *tzedaka*h than we do on obtaining food, water and clothing: things that are basic necessities of life (Matthew

6:31-34). In one place Yeshua even pronounces a blessing over those who have a hunger and thirst for righteousness or *tzedakah*. However, Yeshua is not the only one who spoke of the significance of *tzedakah* (or righteousness) as the priority of Scripture, look at what the Apostle Paul had to say about the matter:

> *"All Scripture is given by inspiration of God, and is profitable for doctrine, reproof, for correction, for instruction in righteousness, that the man of God may be thoroughly equipped for every good work."* **2 Timothy 2:16-17**

According to Apostle Paul, every Scripture that was written under the inspiration of the Holy Spirit is given to us so that we could be taught (doctrine), given evidence or proof for (reproof), be rectified and reformed in (correction), and tutored and trained (instruction) in righteousness (*tzedakah*) so that we may also be thoroughly equipped to do good works or the works of God.

By the way I didn't forget the fact that the Apostle Paul said that it is profitable, or lucrative in terms of potential gain for us, to learn to work righteousness or *tzedakah*. A discussion on the profitability of laboring in *tzedakah as it relates to your faith* comes later, so keep reading because you don't want to miss that discussion.

UNDERSTANDING TZEDAKAH

So what is *tzedakah*? The traditional and contemporary idea of righteousness in Christianity is that it means right standing with God, and that it's a position that one receives strictly because of his belief in Yeshua. Based on this definition, it is usually deemed that one is righteous because they believe, and not because of what they do. The problem with this definition of righteousness is that it is not a complete or accurate translation of the word we are trying to understand here, which is *"tzedakah."* Contrary to the predominant Christian understanding of righteousness, *tzedakah* has everything to do with works. In fact, even though it may sound taboo according to some denominations, *tzedakah* (i.e. righteousness) is about your **GOOD WORKS!**

Righteousness is actually something you *work!* Please do not confuse righteousness with justification. It is justification that we have received by grace, which has nothing to do with good works, but only God's goodness (Romans 4:25; 5:16). Furthermore, as we make this important distinction between righteousness (tzedakah) and justification (tzedak), it is important that we understand that we are not teaching or endorsing a salvation that is based on works. It is only the Messiah who has delivered and freed us from the guilt and penalty of our sins. And as a result of God's grace and what He alone has done, having shouldered the consequence of our sin, we are innocent of sin through Him. However, just because we are innocent of any wrong doing (sin), does not make us guilty of doing good. This is the difference between being justified and being righteous. Being justified means we have been judged as blameless, but being righteous implies that we are guilty of doing good.

WHY THE CONFUSION?

Part of the confusion or misunderstanding of these important words and concepts is due to the fact that both the words for righteousness and being justified have the same root in both Hebrew and Greek. In Hebrew the root is tzedek (צדק) and in

Greek the root is dikaios (δίκαιος). Obviously this is worthy of a full study in and of itself, which we will not expound on in this text, but I thought it was important that you have at least an introduction to understanding the root and origin of these words and how they can be translated and still possibly misinterpreted. Our focus in this particular work is not tzedek or being justified, but Tzedakah, which is a reflection of the good that we do in demonstration of our love to God and to one another. And is a measure of our good works, which attract the blessings of the Kingdom and in fact cultivates the culture of the Kingdom in our sphere of influence.

Hopefully, you understand going forward that as we discuss tzedakah (righteous) we are not speaking of something that you must do to be saved, but something you do that is evidence that you truly are a follower of the Messiah. As you study the scriptures you will discover that your tzedakah is the key to God's blessings being unleashed on you in this life. With that being stated here are a few scriptures below (emphasis added) to confirm and establish the idea that *tzedakah* (righteousness) is something you do or work (for).

"LORD, who may abide in Your tabernacle? Who may dwell in Your holy hill? He who walks uprightly, and <u>works</u> righteousness, and speaks the truth in his heart." **Psalm 15:1-2**

"The wicked man does deceptive <u>work</u>, but he who <u>sows</u> righteousness will have a sure reward." **Proverbs 11:18**

"You meet him who rejoices and <u>does</u> righteousness..." **Isaiah 64:5**
"But in every nation whoever fears Him and <u>works</u> righteousness is accepted by Him." **Acts 10:35**

"The <u>work</u> of righteousness will be peace and the effect of righteousness, quietness and assurance forever." **Isaiah 32:17**

"If you know that He is righteous, you know that everyone who <u>practices</u> righteousness is born of Him." **1 John 2:29**

"Little children, let no one deceive you. He who <u>practices</u> righteousness is righteousness, just as He is righteous." **1 John 3:7**

"In this the children of God and the children of the devil are manifest: Whoever does not <u>practice</u> righteousness is not of God, nor is he who does not love his brother." **1 John 3:10**

"Blessed are those who keep justice and he who <u>does</u> righteousness at all times." **Psalm 106:3**
"Then it will be righteousness for us, if we are careful to observe all these commandments before the LORD our GOD, as He has commanded us."
Deuteronomy 6:25

Obviously these Scriptures speak of righteousness as something that we work or do. The Apostle John put it plainly when he stated that he who does or practices righteousness is righteous. Yet, I realize that many people may still struggle to come to that understanding based on those Scriptures alone, so let's go into a more detailed explanation of *tzedakah*.

A KINGDOM CONUNDRUM

There are a few challenges to properly understanding tzedakah, which we will now discuss discuss. The first challenge is that the scriptures speak of two different facets of tzedakah or righteousness, both of which we must understand as citizens of the Kingdom of God. The first facet of righteousness is revealed in the context of the previous scripture (Deuteronomy 6:25), which is that our observance of God's commandments are in fact a measure of our degree of righteousness before God. In other words, the more a person seeks to obey God the more righteous they are before God. To confirm this idea, take a look at scripture below that speaks of John the Baptist's parents as righteous in relation to God's commandments.

"And they were both righteous before God, walking in all the commandments and ordinances of the Lord blameless." **Luke 1:6**

This first facet of tzedakah or righteousness is what we will refer to as vertical tzedakah, which is key to our relationship to God and level in the Kingdom. However, obedience to the commandments of God are not only a measure of or righteousness. Look at what Yeshua said about the importance of obedience to God's commandments.

"He who has My commandments and keeps them, it is he who loves Me. And he who loves Me will be loved by My Father, and I will love him and manifest Myself to him." **John 14:21**

"If you love Me, keep My commandments." **John 14:15**

In both the previous scriptures Yeshua reveals that our love of God is also measured by our obedience to His commandments. Later we will discuss the connection between love and tzedakah for now it is important that you understand there is a relationship between the two.

The second and probably main challenge that many have had in understanding *tzedakah* is that it has no English equivalent. In other words, there is not one word that we can use to translate the idea of *tzedakah* into the English language. *Tzedakah* does not equal righteousness, it is much more. The third challenge believers have with accurately understanding *tzedakah* is that it is such a strange word in that it is an oxymoron. It encompasses two seemingly contradictory ideas, one of charity (or generosity) and the other justice. Trying to understand it is like trying to understand the idea of deafening silence, or bitter sweetness. This is the second facet of tzedakah, which deals with acts of charity and generosity toward our neighbors. Interestingly, when we put both facets of tzedakah together (both vertical and horizontal tzedakah) it forms a cross.

THE JUSTICE OF GENEROSITY

So how can the word *tzedakah* mean both charity (i.e. generosity) and justice? Although the word *tzedakah* is more accurately translated as charity it comes from the Hebrew root word "*tzedek*", which means justice. This is what makes it such a strange word, how can something be justice and charity at the same time? If I owe you something it is not charity when I give it to you, it is justice. Conversely, if I give you something that I did not owe you out of the desire of my heart to be kind and generous, then it is not justice--it is charity (or generosity).

This gets even more interesting when you look closely at the meaning of the words, charity and justice. The word "charity," is from the Latin word *"caritas,"* and means a generous donation or gift given out of love and kindness to help the poor, the sick, and others in need. Charity can involve giving money, food, water, clothes, time and energy (volunteering) or other resources to help out with a particular need.

On the other hand, the word justice means to do what is right or lawful. So you see, *tzedakah* can be translated as righteousness, but only in the sense that it means to do what is right or lawful. At best, the word righteousness is only a third of the definition of *tzedakah*. Fully translated *tzedakah* means to act charitably (or generously), to act in loving kindness and to act justly towards your neighbor (Micah 6:8).

THE ROYAL LAW

"If you really fulfill the royal law according to the Scripture, You shall love your neighbor as yourself, you do well." **James 2:8**

In the Kingdom of God *tzedakah* is the idea that it is just (right and lawful) to act in love, and kindness towards others. Therefore, *tzedakah* is the method for fulfilling what James calls the "Royal Law," to love your neighbor as you love yourself. So how do you reconcile these two words into one to make the word *tzedakah*? In God's eyes, when you have the opportunity to help someone in need when you can, God considers it lawful for you to do so.
Even if all you're able to do is pray for an individual in need of assistance, it is not only good to do so it is just and right. Look at the following scripture below where Samuel states the significance of not praying for those in need of your prayers:

"And all the people said to Samuel, pray for your servants to the LORD your God, that we may not die; for we have added to all our sins the evil of asking a king for ourselves... Then Samuel said to the people, do not fear... Moreover, as for me, far be it from me that I should sin against the LORD in ceasing to pray for you; but I will teach you the good and the right way." **1 Samuel 12:19-23**

How interesting, that God considers it sin, for those who are able, to forfeit praying for those in need? I know some may be wondering how, or if sin is related to acting unlawfully or out of compliance with Kingdom law. Absolutely! The Hebrew word commonly used for sin is the word *"chattath,"* which means to miss the mark, but it also means an offense (to the law). The Apostle John said it this way: "He who commits sin also commits lawlessness, and sin is lawlessness" **1 John 3:4**.

In other words, sin is acting outside of the law or what is lawful in the Kingdom of God. In reference to *tzedakah* (righteousness), that means that every time we have neglected to pray for or help those we could, God considered us as being out of compliance with Kingdom law. Here are a few Scriptures to remind us that God wants us to do good and be conscious of opportunities to do good:

"Do not withhold good from those to whom it is due, when it is in the power of your hand to do so." **Proverbs 3:27**

"Therefore, as we have opportunity, let us do good to all, especially to those who are of the household of faith." **Galatians 6:10**

"Let them do good, that they be rich in good works, ready to give, willing to share, storing up for themselves a good foundation for the time to come, that they may lay hold on eternal life."
1 Timothy 6:18

"But do not forget to do good and to share, for with such sacrifices God is well pleased." **Hebrews 13:16**

"Therefore, to him who knows to do good and does not do it, to him it is sin." **James 4:17**

I think Solomon summed the Idea of our moral obligation and lawful duty to do *tzedakah* when he stated, "Do not withhold good from those to whom it is due, when it is in the power of your hand to do so" (Proverbs 3:27). In other words, when you are aware of an opportunity for you to help someone in need and you are in position to help, you owe it to them to help.

Now this is not to make anyone feel condemned, because there is no condemnation to those who are in Christ Yeshua. Yet, it is to remind us that God judges us based on His law that also includes us doing good to those whom it is in our power to help. Below are just a few Scriptures to remind us that God is going to judge us according to our works.

"...because He has appointed a day on which He will judge the world in righteousness by the Man whom He has ordained..." **Acts 17:31**

"...and revelation of the righteous judgment of God, who will render to each one according to his deeds." **Romans 2:5-6**

"And behold, I am coming quickly, and My reward is with Me, to give to everyone according to his work." **Revelation 22:12**

DEVELOPING RIGHTEOUSNESS CONCIOUSNESS

After reading these Scriptures, I hope you have been inspired to be more conscious of doing good or pursuing *tzedakah*. We are not to casually do good, but we must be intentional about seeking *tzedakah* opportunities. If you miss an opportunity to do an act of righteousness (*tzedakah*), thankfully, God will forgive you.

"If we confess our sins, He is faithful and just to forgive us our sins and to cleanse us from all unrighteousness." **1 John 1:9**

Take a moment to consider if perhaps you need to repent (turn and change your ways) for neglecting opportunities to do good for those you could have helped. Maybe, you have neglected your obligation to do *tzedakah* in prayer, or financially, or volunteering, or ignoring the homeless man, etc... If so, you may want to read, meditate on and repeat the following prayer:

"Dear Father,
I have come to realize the significance of ignoring or neglecting opportunities for me to do good to others. I now understand that you are glorified and honored through the good works we do for one another. I ask that you would forgive me for all unrighteousness, and for not loving my neighbor as I love myself. I ask that you would help me to better understand how to have a righteousness consciousness and to teach me how to walk in righteousness. Thank you for hearing and answering me. Amen."

Chapter 3 Power Points

- The primary objective of scripture is to equip us to be workers of righteousness.
- Righteousness, is not about your belief in the Messiah, but it is about demonstrating your love to God through obedience and about demonstrating love to your neighbors through acting charitably and generously towards others.
- We must be intentional about seeking opportunities to do tzedakah, and have a mindset to do good for those when we have the occasion to do so.

CHAPTER 4
DEFINING REAL KINGDOM LOVE

"If you really fulfill the royal law according to the Scripture, You shall love your neighbor as yourself, you do well." **James 2:8**

What does *tzedakah* have to do with love and the fulfilling of the royal law? Well, we have already defined *tzedakah* as best as we could. Now let us take a look at God's idea of love to see the connection between the two.

Traditionally, the church has defined love using the Greek word "agape," which describes God as having unconditional love. While it is true that God has unconditional love for us, when Yeshua stated the two greatest commandments He quoted two verses from the Hebrew Scriptures which read as follows:

"Hear, O Israel: The LORD our God, the LORD is one! You shall love the LORD your God with all your heart, with all your soul and with all your strength." **Deuteronomy 6:4**

"You shall not take vengeance, nor bear any grudge against the children of your people, but you shall love your neighbor as yourself: I am the LORD." **Leviticus 19:18**

So what is my point? Well, the word used for love in these scriptures is not the Greek word for love - agape, but a Hebrew word for love. So what's the big deal? Isn't love defined the same way in any language? No. As a matter of fact, if you ask ten different people to define love, you may end up with ten different answers. So what is the Hebrew word for love?

"AHAV"

אהב

The word *ahav* does mean to love, but it is more specific as to **how** we are to love. The word a*hav*, comes from the Hebrew root word "*hav*," which means... "To **<u>GIVE.</u>**" Before you read on, I would like you to pause for a moment and think about this as God's definition of love...

The world may define love as an emotion, or feeling, but God defines love as giving. This means that the truest measure of your love for someone or something is not how much you feel for them, but how much you give and are willing to give towards that person or thing. This is what Yeshua had in mind when He stated the following:

> *"For where your treasure is, there your heart will be also."*
> **Matthew 6:21**

In other words, Yeshua was also stating that what you give to is really what you love. With that in mind your bank ledger and financial transactions can be one of the best ways to measure who or what you love most. Take a look at your bank ledger, does it show that you love your neighbors like you love yourself? Before we go any further, and while you are thinking about how your giving reflects your love in God's eyes, let's take a look at a few Scriptures that speak of or measure love, in terms of giving.

> *"For God so loved the world that He gave His only begotten Son, that whoever believes in Him should not perish but have everlasting life."* **John 3:16**

"Husbands, love your wives, just a Christ also loved the church and gave Himself for her." **Ephesians 5:25**

"Greater love has no one than this, than to lay down one's life for his friends" **John 15:13**

"In this the love of God was manifested toward us, that God has sent His only begotten Son into the world, that we might live through Him" **1 John 4:9**

"Since you were precious in My sight, You have been honored, and I have loved you; therefore I will give men for you, and people for your life." **Isaiah 43:4**

Now I've only given you a few Scriptures that speak of love in terms of giving, but the fact of the matter is that Yeshua talked more about money than heaven and hell combined. Isn't that interesting? Especially when you consider that many people, including believers, are turned off or offended when a minister of the gospel, begins talking about giving. Usually, this same group of people who are offended when the minister representing God asks them to give, doesn't seem to think God is offended, by all of their frequent personal requests of God's gifts and generosity. Don't you think it strange for someone to think it's okay to expect God to give to them, but think it's a perversion of the Gospel for God to ask you to give? If you are irritated by conversations about money in relation to the Gospel, then you probably would have had issues attending Yeshua's meetings or Bible studies if you were there two thousand years ago. For instance Yeshua told people to sell what they had and give to the poor before following Him (Matthew 19:21).

You're probably likely to be turned off by the Torah or what many Christians refer to as the Old Testament. Think about the many offerings and gifts God required the people to give in the Torah. In the book of Leviticus alone there are over 200 references to giving (or offerings). Why? What is so significant about offerings? Does God really need us to give that much? Well, I'm sure some of you already have it figured out or are beginning to see the connection. Remember in God's eyes, your love for someone is measured by what you give and also by how much you give. As a matter of fact, one of the Hebrew words frequently used for offering is the word "**korban**", which does mean an offering, but even more accurately it means to draw near, to approach, or to be at hand. In other words, our closeness to God is also measured by how much we give for His sake.

DOES GOD WANT YOUR MONEY?

At the risk of sounding sacrilegious, I'll say, YES! God wants your money. Why? Because He knows if He has your money, He has your heart. So to put it more accurately, God really wants your heart. It just so happens that who or what has your money is the best measure of who or what has your heart. Remember the words of Yeshua, *"Where your treasure is, there your heart will be also."* (**Matthew 6:21**). Let me show you why your love is measured by your giving.

You, having one life to live and one body to live it out (in this age or world), will go and work forty or more hours a week, trading your strength, and time you will never have again in order to get money. So, in essence you are trading a portion of your life for money. **This** means that when you give your hard earned money it is as if you are giving a portion of your life, since you already traded precious time of your life for the money you earned. So, if you earn $10/hr and you give $100 to feed starving children, you didn't just give $100 to feed the children, but in addition and more significantly you gave 10 hours of your life so those children would not starve... Wait, please re-read that one more time.

Now think about what I just said and take a minute to think about your salary or hourly pay. If you are a person who tithes regularly throughout the year, meaning you give 10% of your income to the church or some charity, that means you didn't just give a tax deductible dollar amount. Let me show you how I believe God measures your gift with the formula below.

hrs. of work per week____ x 52wks/yr – weeks of vacation___ =hrs of work/yr__ x 10% =__

Let's make more sense of this formula by plugging in some numbers:

The average American works 40 hours per week, and there are 52 weeks in a year. This equals 2080 hours. Subtract from that the 2 weeks of vacation, which the average American worker gets per year and you are left with around 2000 hours the average American works in a year. Regardless of how much money they earn in a year, they earn it in about 2000 hours. If that person then gives 10% of their income to church or a charity, God does not just see it as if they gave 10% of their income to a needy cause, but as if they traded 10% or 200 hours of their life for something they love.

Now do you see why giving *tzedakah* (financially) is so highly esteemed in the sight of God? You don't just give your money, you give your life. This is also what is intended by this proverb: *"He who follows righteousness and mercy finds life, righteousness and honor."* **(Proverbs 21:21)** Your gifts of *tzedakah* not only bring you closer to

God, but it's you pursuing life. This is how God gave eternal life to those who believe. He didn't just give His son to show His love (**John 3:16**), but He took the life of His Son, which is eternal, and traded it to you in exchange for your faith in Him.

THE KINGDOM IS KORBAN

By the way, remember earlier I explained that the word frequently used for offering, "korban," also means to draw near or be at hand? Well, when Yeshua was speaking to a group of Hebrews about the Kingdom, He would not have said, the "Kingdom of Heaven is at hand" (Matthew 4:17). No way! That's English, and I'm pretty sure He didn't speak to them in English, but He most likely spoke to a Hebrew audience in the Hebrew language. So how would Yeshua have proclaimed the Kingdom of Heaven to be at hand? It's possible that He would have said that the Kingdom of Heaven was **"KORBAN!"** In other words, He would have been not only saying that the Kingdom was near, but that the Eternal King and His Kingdom was now being offered (*korban*) to you as a gift from God. To put it another way, the Kingdom of Heaven is God's offering to you. This is also what Yeshua had in mind when He stated the following:

> *"Do not fear, little flock, for it is our Father's good pleasure to give you the Kingdom."*
> **Luke 12:32**

Now do you see the connection between *tzedakah* and love? To love is to give and to give *tzedakah* is to give generously or charitably with the mindset that it is just for you to give when you can. Simply put, *tzedakah* is demonstrating your love towards others (through giving).

LOVE IS RECIPROCAL

Before we continue our discussion of *tzedakah*, let me explain something else about love and that is that love is reciprocal. This means that **whatever we love, we give to (or for), but it also works the opposite way, in that whatever we give to will also come to be what we love**. So when God commands us to love our neighbors as we love ourselves, He is not asking that we feel the same level of emotion or feeling for our neighbors as we feel for a spouse or immediate family members. However, in commanding us to love our neighbors, He is asking us to give to our neighbors like we give to and love ourselves. So how do you give to (i.e. love) yourself? Well for starters, when you are hungry, you give yourself something to eat, so you should give to your neighbor something to eat when they are hungry. When you are thirsty, you give yourself something to drink, so you should give your neighbor something to drink when they are thirsty. When you are sick, you give attention and care to yourself, so when your neighbor is sick you should visit and help care for them.

     Obviously, we could extend this list for several pages, but the point is that the command to love your neighbor also known as the royal law, is about giving to them when they're in need and you are in a position to help.

A PICTURE OF LOVE

אהב

We have already defined love with words, now for the fun part of defining love according to the Hebrew pictograph. The *"aleph"* is a picture of an ox and represents strength, leader or first. The *"hey"* is a picture of a window and represents revealing or beholding or looking after. The *"beit"* is a picture of a tent, and represents a household. Do you see the picture yet? Together *"ahav,"* **is a picture of using one's strength or resources to look after a household.** To put it directly to you, your love can be clearly seen and known by or in what you exert your strength and resources to look after.

Obviously, you could love and look after a number of things, but let's now look at a few Scriptures that speak of what or who we are to look after or show love to.

"If one of your brethren becomes poor, and falls into poverty among you, then you shall help him, like a stranger or a sojourner, that he may live with you." **Leviticus 25:35**

"If there is among you a poor man of your brethren, within any of the gates in your land which the LORD your God is giving you, you shall not harden your heart nor shut your hand from your poor brother, but you shall open your hand wide to him and willingly lend him sufficient for his need whatever he needs." **Deuteronomy 15:7-8**

> *"For the poor will never cease from the land; therefore I command you, saying, you shall open your hand wide to your brother, to your poor and your needy, in your land."* **Deuteronomy 15:11**

> *"Is this not the fast I have chosen: To loose the bonds of wickedness, to undo the heavy burdens, to let the oppressed go free, and that you break every yoke? Is it not to share your bread with the hungry, and that you bring to your house the poor who are cast out; When you see the naked, that you cover him, and not hide yourself from your own flesh?"* **Isaiah 58:6-7**

THE FATHER'S LABOR OF LOVE

I'm not sure if you noticed not only the connection between the words *tzedakah* and love, which are both centered on giving, but the interesting connection between the words father and love? Remember, a father is one who upholds or sustains a household, and to love is to give or utilize your strength and resources to look after and care for a household. This is the work of the Father. He is in the business of giving His all, His resources, and strength to look after and lift up His house and family. This is not only the work of the Father, but it is who He is. He is a giver, but not a casual one. He diligently seeks opportunities to assist, enlighten, empower and support those in need of help.

> *"Do not fear, little flock, for it is your Father's good pleasure to give you the kingdom."* **Luke 12:32**

This is the essence of the gospel of the Kingdom. The Omnipotent and Eternal King has made all the resources of His Kingdom available to earth. And not only are the resources available, but we are told that it is His *good pleasure* to give us the Kingdom!

CHAPTER 4 POWER POINTS

- In the Kingdom of God love is not defined or measure by feeling or emotion, but it is defined and evident by how much one gives of themselves and their resources.
- Giving brings the giver and the receiver closer together. This is the reason God talks so much about offerings and gifts, because it is the evidence of love.
- The only proof that we love is that we give, this is why Yeshua taught that your heart is with your money and resources (or treasures).

CHAPTER 5
DO YOU KNOW THE HEAVENLY FATHER?

"O righteous Father! The world has not known You, but I have known You; and these have known that You sent Me." **John 17:25**

The previous question is so important, that I will repeat it, because if nothing else, the answer to that question and how to know the Father is worth your time reading this book if nothing else is. So, here it is again… Do you know the Father? Later, we will ask you if the Father knows *you*, but for now let's focus on what it means to know the Father.

Before you answer that question, I want you to think about what it means to know someone. Do you know someone because you heard about them or even because you read about them in a book or magazine? What is the prerequisite for being able to say that you know someone? More importantly, what are God's qualifications for someone being able to truly say that they know Him? The Hebrew word for knowing someone is *"yada"*, and it means to know through seeing, observing, and understanding. It is knowledge that is gained through experience and observation. Thankfully we don't have to calculate if we know God based on our own understanding or opinions. Through the prophet Jeremiah, God explains exactly what it means to know Him. Please read the following Scripture closely, especially if you would like to truly know God.

> *"Did not your father eat and drink, and do justice and righteousness? Then it was well with him. He judged the cause of the poor and needy; Then it was well. Was not this knowing Me? Says the LORD."* **Jeremiah 22:15-16**

Was the previous verse clear to you? Have you ever seen it before? Who knew that the key to understanding what it means to truly know God was right there in Scripture? What really surprised me about this Scripture is what is *not* mentioned. God did not saying that reading or memorizing all of Scripture was equivalent to knowing Him. He didn't say that if you really had a strong belief that He exists, that you know Him. Neither did He say that regularly attending church or some religious service was equal to knowing Him. So what did He say was equivalent to knowing Him? To do justice and righteousness (*tzedakah*), and to judge the cause of the poor and needy. Unfortunately, the statement about judging the cause of the poor and needy does not really give an accurate idea of this Scripture. This does not mean that we should sit back and use our own judgment to try and determine the cause or reason for the poor or needy person being in their situation. This may be a surprise to some, but God is not interested in His people <u>only</u> identifying and discussing the issues of our neighbors and communities.

So what is a more accurate meaning of this Scripture? The word translated as "judge" is the Hebrew word "*din*" (דִּין), which of course means to judge. However, as you've probably already guessed it means much more. So let's look at the Hebrew pictograph for the word judge.

ARE YOU A JUDGE?

The Hebrew word for judge, "**din**" is formed with letters *dalet* and *nun*. The *dalet* is a picture of an open door and represents access, entry or a pathway. And *nun* is a picture of fish and represents multiplication, activity or life. Combined, these give the picture that a judge is one who opens the door to life. In ancient Hebrew culture, the concept of a judge was one whose purpose was to help establish and or restore a peaceful life to the people. This is also what God had in mind when He spoke through the psalmist Asaph in the following Scripture:

> "How long will you judge unjustly, and show partiality to the wicked? Selah. Defend the poor and fatherless; Do justice to the afflicted and needy. Deliver the poor and needy; Free them from the hand of the wicked." **Psalm 82:2-4**

If the ancient Hebrew idea of a judge is one that open the door to life for others, we probably need to know who it is that we are to judge. To understand this concept a little better, let's examine the individuals referred to in the Scripture above.

The word translated poor in the verse above is the word *"dal"*, and refers to those who are so weak and feeble that they are dangling or just barely holding on to life. The word "fatherless," is the Hebrew word *"yathom"*, and of course it means one without a father, but it also means to be lonely, left alone, or bereaved. "Afflicted," is the word *"aniy"*, and refers to one who is hurt or depressed and humiliated, due to being poor or impoverished. And lastly, the word for "needy" is the word *"rush"*, which also means to be destitute. These are those who lack basic necessities for life. The Hebrew pictograph for the needy (*"rush"*) is very graphic in meaning. It is formed of two letters, the first is *"resh,"* which is a picture of a head and represents a person, leadership, or highest authority. The second letter forming the word for needy is *"shin,"* which is a picture of teeth, and represents consuming or destroying. Together, this forms a picture of a needy person as someone who is being consumed or eaten. These are individuals who will be devoured unless someone comes to their aid. Interestingly, in 1 Peter 5:8 it states that the devil goes about like a roaring lion seeking whom he may devour, and it is they who judge others with the heart and mind of God, who deliver others from the roaring lions.

I frequently hear people say that we are not supposed to judge others. Yet God calls us to act as judges, whose objective is not to condemn people to death, but rather to work to exonerate and liberate others from oppression, depression and destitution (Isaiah 61). In that context you are to embrace your duty and obligation to judge to make the best decisions as to how you are able to help to poor and the needy. This is what it means to know God, to make decisions and actively work to open the doors of life to those in need of our help.

DOES GOD KNOW YOU?

The idea of knowing someone is also reciprocal in its meaning. In other words, if you know someone, then it is also true that they know you. This means that it is not just important to think we know God, but it is more important that He knows us. Interestingly, in the gospel of Matthew, Yeshua explains that there are many people involved in ministry or other religious activities who will not enter the Kingdom of Heaven, because He doesn't know them. Take a look at the Scripture below:

"Not everyone who says to Me, Lord, Lord, shall enter the kingdom of heaven, but he who does the will of My Father in heaven. Many will say to Me in that day, Lord, Lord, have we not prophesied in Your name, cast out demons in Your name, and done many wonders in Your name? And then I will declare to them, I never knew you; depart from Me, you who practice lawlessness." **Matthew 7:21-23**

The reason Yeshua gives for not knowing this group of individuals hoping to enter the Kingdom of God is that they practiced lawlessness. Interestingly, the Greek word translated lawlessness is the word *"anomia,"* which means illegally, and <u>unrighteousness</u>. This word for unrighteousness is the opposite of righteousness (or *tzedakah)* in the Greek. So it's not just that these individuals rejected God's law in general, but it specifically speaks to the fact they rejected the royal law, that commands we act justly and in righteousness towards our neighbors by helping those we have the opportunity to help. **In other words, these individuals were not known to God, because they did not know the poor and needy**.

Are there any other examples of Yeshua teaching that He truly knows those who help the needy and that He does not know and will therefore reject those who neglect or reject those in need? Well...read the following scripture and you decide.

"When the Son of Man comes in His glory, and all the holy angels with Him, then He will sit on the throne of His glory. All the nations will be gathered before Him, and He will separate them one from another, as a shepherd divides his sheep from the goats. And He will set the sheep on His right hand, but the goats on the left. Then the King will say to those on His right hand, come, you blessed of My Father, inherit the kingdom prepared for you from the foundation of

the world: for when I was hungry and you gave me food; I was thirsty and you gave me drink; I was a stranger and you took Me in; I was naked and you clothed Me; I was sick and you visited Me; I was in prison and you came to Me. Then the righteous will answer Him, saying, Lord when did we see you hungry and feed You, or thirsty and give You drink? When did we see You a stranger and take You in, or naked and clothe You? Or when did we see You sick, or in prison and come to You? And the King will answer and say to them, assuredly, I say to you, in as much as you did it to one of the least of these My brethren, you did it to Me. Then He will also say to those on the left hand, Depart from Me, you cursed, into the everlasting fire prepared for the devil and his angels; for I was hungry and you gave Me no food; I was thirsty and you gave Me no drink; I was a stranger and you did not take Me in, naked and you did not clothe Me, sick and in prison and you did not visit Me. Then they also will answer Him, saying Lord, when did we see You hungry or thirsty or a stranger or naked or sick or in prison, and did not minister to You? Then He will answer them, saying, assuredly, I say to you, in as much as you did not do it to one of least of these, you did not do it to Me. And these will go away into everlasting punishment, but the righteous into eternal life." **Matthew 25:31-46**

It is interesting that so much of what many "religious" people consider to be vital to know God and gain eternal life is not even mentioned here. Yeshua did not talk about those entering the Kingdom who possessed great faith in God, or who those who attended church regularly, or those who have memorized much Scripture. Instead, He mentions those who helped their neighbors when they were in need. Wow! How true it is that God's thoughts are not our thoughts and that His ways are not like our ways (Isaiah 55:8-9).

TRUE RELIGION

I pray that this is a wakeup call to many who think that true religion is about appearing holy, or attending church services or reading the Bible faithfully, etc... Many Christians and people of other religious faiths think that God wants us to be primarily concerned with other people's souls, while we focus on our own material needs. This is not God's idea of religion or spirituality, but man's. True spirituality is about being concerned with the total wellbeing of others, beginning with their physical welfare. In other words, it is more spiritual for you to focus on others emotional and material needs, and your own soul, than to focus on others souls and your own emotional and material need. However, don't take my word for it; take a look at what James, the brother of Yeshua, taught as the essence of true religion:

"Pure and undefiled religion before God and the Father is this: to visit orphans and widows in their trouble, and to keep oneself unspotted from the world."(James 1:27)

If this is not clear to you let me put it more plainly. Many "religious" people measure their spiritual condition, by things like prayer, reading the Bible, attending church, and not participating in obvious ungodly activities. While these are important and should not be neglected, according to Scripture there is a better way to measure our spiritual status. Let me explain. Prayer is vitally important and we should be engaged in prayer frequently, it is greater to actually feed the hungry than to pray for the hungry. And it is greater to visit the sick than pray for the sick. And it is greater to visit the prisoners than to pray for the prisoners. And it is greater to give water to the thirsty than to pray for the thirsty.

What do I mean by saying it is greater to give food to the hungry than to pray for the hungry? I mean that it can be of more value and significance to the hungry person to have food to eat than your prayers. This is also what the apostle John had in mind when he made the following statement:

"But whoever has this world's goods, and sees his brother in need, and shuts up his heart from him, how does the love of God abide in him? My little children let us not love in word or in tongue, but in deed and in truth." **1 John 3:17-18**

Indeed, prayer is significant and has its place. But there is a time for everything. When your neighbor is hungry, or thirsty or naked or sick and you have the resources and ability to aid them, it is time to help. But if you are unable to assist with these needs, then pray. Think about it. When the crowds following Yeshua were hungry, did He just say feed them or did He instruct them to pray first (Mark 6:30-42)? Pay close attention, God does not want you to ask Him to do for yourself or others what you can do.

WHO KNOWS GOD?

So is there anyone who the Scripture says knew God or that God knew? Yes, not only did Abraham know God, but he was called a friend of God. Read the following Scriptures to see for yourself.

"Are you not our God, who drove out the inhabitants of this land before Your people Israel, and gave it to the descendants of Abraham Your friend forever." **2 Chronicles 20:7**

"But you, Israel, are My servant, Jacob whom I have chosen, the descendants of Abraham My friend." **Isaiah 41:8**

"And the Scripture was fulfilled which says, Abraham believed God, and it was accounted to him for righteousness. And he was called the friend of God." **James 2:23**

It is interesting to note that the word used in both 2 Chronicles 20, and Isaiah 41 to describe Abraham as God's friend, is not the traditional Hebrew word for friend, which is *"reya,"* but is the word *"ahav,"* which again is the word for love. This teaches us that Abraham was not just a friend of God in the sense of being an associate of His, but that he was a friend who God loved deeply. Although the previous Scriptures clearly state that Abraham knew God and was even considered to be a friend of God, we should also be able to find scriptural proof that records that Abraham did what it took to know God according to Jeremiah 22:16. And what was it again that God says is to know Him? To do justice and righteousness or *tzedakah*. So now all we have to do is find a Scripture where God states that He knows Abraham because He does justice and righteousness. Are you ready? Here it is:

And the LORD said, shall I hide from Abraham what I am doing, since Abraham shall surely become a great and mighty nation, and all the nations of the earth shall be blessed in him? **For I have known him, in order that he may command his children and his household after him, that they keep the way of the LORD to do righteousness and justice,** *that the LORD may bring to Abraham what He has spoken to him."* **Genesis 18:17-19**

Because of potential translations issues, I want you to look a bit closer at a couple of the Hebrew translations in this verse. The first, is the word translated as *"known,"* which is the Hebrew word *"yada,"* and means to know. The second is the word translated as *"in order,"* which is the word *"mahan,"* and it means on account of or because of. In other words, this word *mahan*, is helping the reader to understand WHY God stated He knew Abraham.

So let's read this Scripture again in light of the true meaning of the word *mahan*: *"For I know him, because he commands his children and his household after him, that they keep the way of the LORD, which is to do righteousness and justice."*

Obviously this is consistent with what God says it means to know Him, through the prophet Jeremiah. To do justice and *tzedakah* (righteousness) is how we get to know God. Now after confirming what it means to know God, I will again ask: Do you know God?

CHAPTER 5 POWER POINTS

- God defines those who truly know Him as those who practice tzedakah.
- True religion is ministering to the emotional and material needs of others in need.
- Not those who only call Yeshua LORD shall enter the excel the Kingdom, but those who practice tzedakah.

CHAPTER 6

HOW AND WHY THE LORD KNOWS THE RIGHTEOUS

"For the LORD knows the way of the righteous, but the way of the ungodly shall perish."
Psalms 1:6

It is without hesitation that we can now conclude that the LORD knows the righteous or those who practice *tzedakah* (righteousness). For this reason God professed to know Abraham, and in this way He calls us to know Him. Nevertheless, for the sake of those needing more confirmation that God knows the righteous and the righteous know Him, here is one more Scripture:

"I, the LORD, have called you in righteousness, and will hold your hand..." **Isaiah 42:6**

Let's magnify this scripture a bit more to see if we can get any more clarity and meaning. When you look closer at the Hebrew word translated in this Scripture as *"called,"* you'll see it is the word *"qara"* and it means to call out specifically by name. However, there is more, the word *"qara"* also means *"to encounter"* or *"to have met."*

    Wow! That means when you read this scripture more closely, you'll see that God has called us to meet or encounter Him through doing *tzedakah*. Hence, the more you engage in doing good for others, the more you engage God's presence.

SEEKING HIS RIGHTEOUSNESS

Why is it the righteous that can be truly considered as knowing God and who He Himself identifies with? Let's read the two verses below to see if we can better understand.

"But let him who glories glory in this, that he understands and knows Me, that I am the LORD, exercising loving-kindness, judgment and righteousness in the earth. For in these I delight, says the LORD." **Jeremiah 9:24**
"O Lord, righteousness belongs to You..." **Daniel 9:7**

Do you understand now why the righteous or those who practice *tzedakah* get to know God? His way is the way of righteousness, and *tzedakah* is His possession. This means that when a person operates in *tzedakah,* they are also with God and the more time they spend doing *tzedakah*, the more time they spend with God and consequently, the more they get to know God.

SEEKING HIS FACE

"This is Jacob, the generation of those who seek Him, who seek Your face." **Psalm 24:6**

Have you ever desired to seek the LORD or to seek God's face? What exactly does that mean? Do you know? The real question we should ask is: How does one search to find the LORD? Or, where should we look to find Him?

If one wants to find God the question they should ask is, where is He or where is He most likely to be? If you ask the average believer where you can find God, many would respond by saying He is in Heaven above. This is the reason why when believers set out to seek God's face, they think about going to church or isolating themselves in some secluded place where they can read their Bible and pray for long periods without any interruptions. As a matter of fact, there are groups of people who go away on retreats called encounters, where the goal or idea is that they would have an encounter with God.

So how do we find Him and how do we encounter the Almighty? Does God give us instruction on how to seek Him and how we can encounter Him? Absolutely! Believe it or not God is not playing hide and seek with us. He is not calling out for us to find Him while He hides in some impossible place for us to find Him. As a matter of fact, He is out in the open, in plain sight and has given us instructions on how seek and encounter Him. Thankfully, the beloved David, a man after God's own heart explained how to find God. And here it is:

"As for me, I will see your face in righteousness..." **Psalm 17:15**

Do you now understand how to seek God's face and how to encounter Him? Simply put, David tells us through one of his many inspired Psalms that doing *tzedakah* or following opportunities to do charitable deeds will cause us to see His face. This is also consistent with Isaiah 42:6, which we examined earlier:

"I, the LORD, have called you in righteousness, and will hold your hand..." (Isaiah 42:6)

As we discussed earlier, the word translated "called" is the Hebrew word *"qara,"* which also means to encounter. So there you have it! If you truly want to encounter God and meet Him, you don't have to die. You don't even have to go off to a mountain top for 40 days and 40 nights in seclusion. All you need to do is pursue opportunities to do good and be a blessing to others. Since that is what God Himself is in pursuit of, this is where and how you will find Him.

HEARING HIS VOICE

According to some Jewish rabbis, the way a person becomes sensitive and in tune with hearing the voice of God is by learning to hear the voice of the weak and needy. To put it another way, if you cannot hear those in need, then you may not hear God's voice either. Some Jewish rabbis teach that if you won't hear others in need of help, then God will not hear you when you need His help. We will discuss how your hearing others affects how God hears you later. For now let's look at how Elijah was able to identify and know the voice of God.

"Then He said, Go out, and stand on the mountain before the LORD. And behold, the LORD passed by, and a great and strong wind tore into the mountains and broke the rocks in pieces before the LORD, but the LORD was not in the wind; and after the wind an earthquake, but the LORD was not in the earthquake; and after the earthquake a fire, but the LORD was not in the fire; and after the fire, a still, small voice. So it was, when Elijah heard it, that he wrapped his face in his mantle and went out and stood in the entrance of the cave. Suddenly a voice came to him and said, what are you doing here, Elijah?" **1 Kings 19:11-13**

This particular passage is very interesting. However, the one thing I want to you to take a closer look at are the words translated as "still

and small" as in still, small voice. What do you suppose a still, small voice is? The word for still is the word *"damamah,"* which means "quiet, silenced or cut off." The word translated "small" is the Hebrew word *"dak,"* which means something crushed or beaten very small. Again, many rabbis teach the idea that the voice of God when speaking to mankind sounds like the voice of those who have been beaten or crushed by life. This means that if God wants to speak to you, He may use the voice of someone in need. Ask yourself, "Has God tried to speak to me through the needs of others?" Or, are you too busy looking for Him in the fire?
Here's the bottom line. If you don't practice *tzedakah* (righteousness) by helping the poor and needy, then according to God Himself, you do not know Him. This is the point the Apostle John had in mind when he made the following statement:

"But whoever has this world's goods and sees his brother in need, and shuts up his heart from him, how does the love of God abide in him? My little children, let us not love in word or in tongue, but in deed and in truth. And by this we know that we are of the truth, and shall assure our hearts before Him… Beloved, let us love one another, for love is of God; and everyone who loves is born of God and knows God. He who does not love does not know God, for God is love… And we have known and believed the love God has for us. God is love, and he who abides in love abides in God, and God in him." **1 John 3:17-19; 4:7-8, 16**

I hope as you read the Scripture above you kept in mind that the Hebrew word for love *"ahav"* means to give. With that consideration, the Apostle is explaining that only those whose practice is to love or give to those in need of assistance are the ones who truly know God.

A PICTURE OF THE RIGHTEOUS

"The way of the wicked is an abomination to the LORD, but He loves him who follows righteousness." **Proverbs 15:9**
"He who follows righteousness and mercy finds life, righteousness, and honor." **Proverbs 21:21**

Interestingly, both Scriptures used above speak of the idea of pursuing righteousness. This is a clear indicator that righteousness or *tzedakah* is something that we must seek to attain. What is even more interesting and revealing about how both Scriptures speak of righteousness, is the Hebrew word used in both Scriptures that is translated into English as "follow after" or "pursue." It is the word *"rodief"*, which means "to pursue" something in the strongest sense possible. It means *to pursue something as if one's life depended on it*. Understanding this helps shed more light on why Yeshua said we should not worry about what we will eat or drink, but in the same breath instructs us to focus on seeking *tzedakah*. Even more compelling is the fact that Yeshua never pronounces a blessing over those who seek after food and drink, even though it provides nourishment to sustain our life and vitality. But He **does** pronounce a blessing over those who hunger and thirst after *tzedakah* (Matthew 5:6). Hmmm...? Is God perhaps teaching that *tzedakah* is more important to the sustenance of His Kingdom than food, water, clothing and shelter combined?

"But He answered and said, It is written, "Man shall not live by bread alone, but by every word that proceeds out of the mouth of God." **Matthew 4:4**

Let us go back for a moment to the idea of being a *rodief tzedakah* or one who passionately pursues *tzedakah* (righteousness). Remember earlier when I explained that every Hebrew letter is also a number as well as a picture? Can you guess what the picture of *tzedakah* is? The word is written below in Hebrew, from right to left, in contemporary block letter form. The original Hebrew letters were not in block form, but in pictograph form.

The first letter *tzadi*, is a picture of a fish hook or man lying on his side or crouching down, in a similar manner to how a lion crouches down while in pursuit of its prey. The second letter *dalet*, a picture of a door which can be opened to give someone access to something or to let someone in. The third letter *qof*, a picture of the back of a head, represents the last or the least. The fourth letter *hey*, a picture of window, represents the idea of revealing or revelation. Together, the letters of the word *tzedakah* give a beautiful pictorial illustration of what it means to pursue *tzedakah* (righteousness). The complete image is that of a person crouching down in stealth mode seeking an opportunity to open their doors or a door for the least or needy, which will give them revelation and insight into the nature and culture of Heaven. *Tzedakah* is a picture of pursing an opportunity to be a blessing to someone as if your life depended on it. It is having the mindset that in the Kingdom of God your life is sustained in pursuing opportunities to help others, just as a lion's life is sustained through pursuing and apprehending its prey.

"He who follows righteousness and mercy finds life, righteousness, and honor." **Proverbs 21:21**

THE RIGHTEOUS ARE AS BOLD AS A LION

"The wicked flee when no man pursues; but the righteous are bold as a lion." **Proverbs 28:1**

In the animal kingdom the lion as a predator usually seeks out the smallest or weakest creatures, which it then pursues to consume. In the Kingdom of God, *tzedakah* is the idea of pursuing the least, weakest or needy; not to consume them, but in order strengthen them. Just as in the animal kingdom, the lion uses its keen eyesight to identify certain weaknesses in order to determine its target; in the Kingdom of God the righteous look for weaknesses to eliminate them (the weaknesses) and strengthen the person.

This is the idea Yeshua had in mind when He instructed His followers to seek not only the Kingdom of God, but seek God's righteousness or *tzedakah* (Matthew 6:33). When you read this passage with the true understanding of *tzedakah*, you'll find He was saying that the people of various kingdoms and nations of the world are occupied with seeking to care and provide for their own needs to eat, drink and be clothed, which are basic essentials for life. Meanwhile, citizens of His Kingdom should not be preoccupied with only taking care of their needs. For in the Kingdom, your Father already knows what you need and will take care of them. Therefore you should focus not on how you will eat, drink or be clothed, but on how your neighbor will eat, drink and be clothed. This is *tzedakah*, helping and caring for others as God has taken care of you.

Believers in Christ must understand this! It is not preaching that gives people insight or revelation of the Kingdom of God. It is the acts of *tzedakah* that opens the windows of Heaven.

CHAPTER 6 POWER POINTS

- The more we engage in tzedakah the more we attract and engage the presence of God.
- Like the lion pursues the weakest animals to consume and eliminate them from the Earth, the person who pursues tzedakah also pursues the weak, not to eliminate them, but to strengthen them.
- Unlike the citizens of other nations on the Earth who are in constant pursuit of their own interests and needs, citizens of the Kingdom of Heaven are to be in constant pursuit of opportunities to do tzedakah and be a blessing to others.

CHAPTER 7

ABRAHAM'S TZEDAKAH

"Open my eyes, that I may see wondrous things from Your law."
Psalm 119:18

We have already discussed what *tzedakah* (righteousness) is, and how a person can truly grow in their knowledge of God through practicing *tzedakah*. In addition, we have identified that the Scripture teaches that God knew Abraham because he practiced *tzedakah* (Genesis 18:19). We have also explained that the Hebrew pictograph of *tzedakah* is a picture of a person pursing the weak, the needy or the least to be a blessing to them like their life depended on it. Now, I want to share with you actual examples of how Abraham pursued *tzedakah*. If you believe the Scripture as I do, that Abraham is the father of our faith, then this will transform your life. What I am about to show you from the life of Abraham is the epitome and primary example of the Kingdom way of life prior to Yeshua's example. Once you see the path that is paved with gold, there is no going back. These are wondrous truths that one must look beneath the *peshat* (surface) of the Scriptures to discover. You have read about Abraham, now let's examine the Scriptures in a way that the Holy Spirit can show you a picture of Abraham.

ABRAHAM'S PURSUIT OF TZEDAKAH

"... And you shall be a blessing." **Genesis 12:2**

As we begin our journey to discover how Abraham actually pursued *tzedakah* we have to review the initial Scripture where God calls Abraham in Genesis 12. Here it is:

"Now the LORD had said to Abram; Get out of your country, from your family and from your father's house, to a land that I will show you. I will make you a great nation; I will bless you and make your name great and you shall be a blessing. And I will curse him who curses you and; And in you all the families of the earth shall be blessed. So Abram departed as the LORD had spoken to him..."
Genesis 12:1-4

This Scripture concerning God's call to Abraham has been read and preached for generations and often times the focus is on the fact that Abraham was so blessed by God. And while it is obviously significant that Abraham was indeed blessed by God, I believe that there is something more significant here regarding God's call to Abraham. After God speaks of blessing Abraham he says something that we may read over if we are not careful. What is it God says next? **"YOU SHALL BE A BLESSING."** Yes, this is the same word that is often used when God commands us to specifically obey Him in regard to something. As a matter of fact, this same Hebrew word *"hayah"* is also used in Deuteronomy 5:7, when God commands that we "SHALL" have no other god before Him. Not only does the use of this word *hayah* help us to understand the main idea of this passage (Genesis 12:1-4), but it reveals much more.

The word *"hayah,"* also means "to be" or "to exist to," and it is from the Hebrew root word *"hava,"* which means to breathe. This means that God was telling Abraham that from that time forward, the reason he breathes and exists was to be a blessing to the nations... Let me put that another way; God was telling Abraham that from this time on, his life and very breath depended on his being a blessing to not just his family, but every family and nationality of people on the Earth. Just as a lion will stalk weaker animals to devour every day, in order to sustain its life, Abraham would have to daily pursue opportunities to bless the weak and needy in order to sustain his existence. This is what Yeshua was also trying to teach us in Matthew 6:31 -33. The people of all nations in the world are in pursuit of food, drink and clothing because it sustains their lives, but in the Kingdom of God the citizens are sustained in pursuing and obtaining *tzedakah*.

So now let me ask you a question. If you consider yourself to be a follower of Yeshua (Jesus) and the seed of Abraham, why do you exist? Is your life sustained by bread alone, or is it sustained by doing to will of the Father?

ABRAHAM'S ALTAR

Now that we understand the reason Abraham breathed and existed was to fulfill God's commandment to be a blessing to all nations, let's look below the *peshat* or the surface of scripture. We will get a better picture of the life of Abraham and *how* he fulfilled the purpose for his existence. Continuing from the last Scripture we read regarding God's commandment to Abraham to be a blessing to all the families of the earth:

"Then Abram took Sarai his wife and Lot, his brother's son, and all their possessions that they had gathered, and the people whom they had acquired in Haran and they departed to go to the land of Canaan. So they came to the land of Canaan. Abram passed through the land to the place of Shechem, as far as the terebinth tree of Moreh. And the Canaanites were then in the land. Then the LORD appeared to Abram and said, 'To your descendants I will give

this land.' And there he built an altar to the LORD who had appeared to him.

And he moved from there to the mountain east of Bethel, and he pitched his tent with Bethel on the west and Ai on the east; there he build an altar to the LORD and called on the name of the LORD. So Abram journeyed, going on still toward the south." **Genesis 12:5-9**

In Genesis 12: 1-3, God commands Abraham to be a blessing to all nations and then tells him to go to a land that He would show him and the next we see Abraham arriving in the land of Canaan. While "Canaan" is the name of a place, there is more meaning under the surface (*peshat*) of the name "Canaan." The name "Canaan" is the Hebrew word *"kenehan***,"** which means humiliated or humbled. But he didn't just stop there. Scripture says he continued until he arrived at the city of Shechem. This would be like saying he arrived in the United States and continued until he reached Dallas, Texas. But the word "Shechem" also has more significance than just a name of a city.   The Hebrew word *"shekem,"* actually means shoulder or place of burdens.

Can you picture this place God took Abraham to, after commanding him to be a blessing to all the families of the Earth? Usually Christians have this biblical view of Canaan as this land milk and honey, a place of abundance and prosperity. However, this was not the Canaan that Abraham arrived at in Genesis 12. When Abraham arrived in Canaan, it was a place burdened with humility. In other words, the Canaan Abraham encountered in Genesis 12 looked a lot more like Haiti after the 2010 earthquake, than a land flowing with milk and honey. But what happens next is amazing! Genesis 12: 7- 8 records that Abraham builds an altar and called on the name of the LORD. Okay, I admit on the surface it doesn't really look or sound all that amazing, but let's look beneath the *peshat* or surface of this Scripture.

The word translated as "altar" is from the Hebrew root word *"zabach,"* which means to offer or slaughter an animal. This is significant when you consider the fact that the sacrificed animal was usually eaten and used to provide food, clothing and shelter. With that in mind, let's rewind for a review of what is happening in light of this understanding of an altar and what it was for: Abraham is commanded by God to be a blessing to all nations and God takes him to a place that is burdened with humility; a place experiencing a famine. And he begins to slaughter some of His flock.
We are then told that after building an altar and slaughtering some of his flock, he calls on the name of the LORD. The word translated into English as "called" is the Hebrew word *"qara,"* which as we discussed before means to meet or encounter, but it also means to invite guest.

This means that when Abraham arrived at a place experiencing famine, where people were suffering from hunger, he remembered that his existence was dependent on being a blessing to others, and immediately began feeding people from his own flock. But this also reveals that the way he invoked God's presence was by inviting the hungry and thirsty to come and be nourished. This is Abraham's *tzedakah* and it is the reason that he knew God and God knew him. According to Jewish teachings, the presence of God regularly frequented Abraham's tent. This is because he frequently invited the hungry and needy into his tent.

ABRAHAM'S HOUSEHOLD

One of my goals in this book is that you will truly discover that every jot or tittle in Scripture is significant (Matthew 5:18). Here's another little jot for you: let's investigate the significance of Abraham's name. Actually, we'll start by examining the meaning and significance of his first name "Abram".

In examining the name Abram for more significance, we must remember that a name is significant of who a person is, what they possess and what they do (even for a living). The name Abram is a compound of two Hebrew words. The first is the word *"ab,"* which as we discussed before means father, and is a picture of a tent –pole, or someone who holds up and sustains a household. The second word forming Abram is the Hebrew word *"rum,"* which means to be exalted or lifted high. Something that is high or lifted up can be viewed by many more people, even those from a far off. This means that Abram is a picture of someone who is viewed as a father by many, even those who were far off. In other words, even though Abram and Sarai had no children, which came from their own loins until they were over ninety, Abram was still viewed as a father by many. Who looked at Abram as a father? How many people viewed Abram as father? Scripture gives insight into the size of Abram's household and who looked to him as a father.

> *"And Abram took Sarai his wife, and Lot his brother's son, and all their substance that they had gathered, and the souls that they had gained in Haran. And they went forth to go into the land of Canaan. And they came into the land of Canaan."* **Genesis 12:5**

So we see that Abram "took" Sarai his wife and Lot and departed. The Hebrew word translated "took" is *"laqach,"* which does mean "to take," but it also means "to carry." This is an indicator of Abram's new relationship to his nephew, Lot, who had been orphaned. Especially since the Hebrew word for father *"ab"* is the idea of lifting up and carrying the load of the house. So Abram didn't just take Lot; from that point forward, he carried the *responsibility and weight* of Lot.

Well obviously, that is merely one example of someone who viewed Abram as father, but there are more. In Genesis 14 we are given more insight as to the size of Abram's household:

> *"Now when Abram heard that his brother was taken captive, he armed his three hundred and eighteen trained servants who were born in his own house, and went in pursuit as far as Dan."* **Genesis 14:14**

Wow! Do you know anyone who is raising 318 children in their home? I don't know about you, but the only place I can think of where 318 children are actually being raised is an orphanage. However, before we jump any conclusions yet about Abram and Sarai having an orphanage (which they probably did) let's examine this passage a bit more closely.

The word used or translated as "trained," as in trained servants is a very interesting word. It is the word *"chaniyk"* and on the surface it means "trained." However, this word *chaniyk* is formed from two Hebrew words, *"chazaq,"* which means "to strengthen, cure, help and repair" and the second word is *"yahh,"* which is a shortened or contracted form of the LORD's name of Yehovah. Together this means that these were children that Abram also discipled or trained in the ways of the LORD.

Do we have any confirmation for that? Well, In Genesis 18:19, God says that He knows Abram because He taught his household to keep the way of the LORD (Yehovah) to practice justice and righteousness (*tzedakah*). That means that these 318 were also being discipled by Abram in how to follow the LORD.

Let me ask you another question. Do you know anyone with 318 disciples? I'm not talking about a pastor of a church, who sees the members once or twice a week. I'm referring to someone who personally and intimately fathers 318 individuals on how to walk in the ways of the LORD. The word "born" is the word *"yaliyd"* and it does actually mean born, but it also means "to show lineage to," "to midwife" and "to bear young." This in fact gives the idea that these 318 where children whom Abram was helping to carry and train in the ways of the LORD. So at most Abram and Sarai ran an orphanage, or at the very least, they were foster parents to at least 318 children. I hope you're starting to see why God would choose a man like Abraham.

GOING DEEPER

A fascinating side note is that the word *"rum"* (the second word forming Abram's name) is also the root word of *"terumah"*, which is the word for the offering God reminds His people to give in Malachi 3:8. The *terumah* was the most holy offering, which was taken from the first fruits of all the increase and then lifted high to be offered to the Father. In other words, the *terumah* was a first fruits offering. This means that Abram, was not just the high or exalted father, but he was the *terumah* or first fruits of a nation. This is why he is also called the father of our faith (Romans 4:11).

CHAPTER 7 POWER POINTS

- Abraham pursued tzedakah as if His life depended on it. To Abraham tzedakah was of greater importance that food and water.
- Abraham taught us is that the way to invite God into our home is to invite people into our home we can be a blessing to.
- Abram was called by this name, which means exalted father, because he through his tzedakah upheld many people.

CHAPTER 8
ABRAHAM'S PRAYER FOR TZEDAKAH

"… My Lord if I have now found favor in Your sight, do not pass on by your servant. Please let a little water be brought, and wash your feet and rest yourselves under the tree." **Genesis 18:3-4**

Christians, based on the contemporary understanding of righteousness as being right-standing with God, are more likely to pray that God would make them more righteous. However, based on the true definition of *tzedakah* (righteousness) as doing charitable deeds to demonstrate love and justice (or rightness), we can understand that we should not pray that God would make us righteous, but that He would give us the opportunities to do *tzedakah* and thereby become more righteous.

In the previous passage we see Abraham saying "please let a little water be brought, to wash your feet" (Genesis 18:4). The Hebrew word used here *"na,"* is a word that can be better translated as "I pray." In other words, Abraham was not just asking them to allow him to bring water to wash their feet. He was explaining to them that at that moment his prayer was that God would allow him an opportunity to do an act of *tzedakah* for these men. This kind of prayer makes sense when you recall that Abraham's existence and his very breath was connected to his being a blessing to others.

Wow! How different that is from how most people pray. How many people spend the majority of their time in prayer asking God to fulfill their needs. This is not the way we are to pray. James tells us that the reason many of our prayers are not answered is because they are often focused on our own selfish pleasures or desires (James 4:3). Believe it or not, God does not want you to spend all your time in prayer asking Him to fulfill your requests and desires; instead He wants you to pray for others in your mind and heart. This is what Yeshua was alluding to in teaching that we who are children of the household of God ought not worry about what we will eat, drink or wear, because the Father already knows that we need these things (Matthew 6:28-34). In other words, based on our understanding of *"Abba"* (dear Father), Yeshua was saying that God will sustain and support us without us having to tell Him what we need. My wife and I have small children. I cannot count the number of times they have asked for clothing, shoes, or food. In fact, from time to time they tell my wife they are hungry *while she is cooking!* You can imagine her reaction...Get out of the kitchen and wait! I know you're hungry. That's why I am preparing a meal!

Interestingly, there are many believers who have given up on the idea of prayer being something that consistently works or produces the desired results. These are people who haven't seen God answer their prayers that mainly benefit their own self interests and have decided it is not worth their time. However, if those same individuals would make a list of people and situations to pray for, and even more significantly, would pray that God give them opportunities to do tzedakah, they would find their prayers heard and answered in an overwhelming manner.

Two more Scriptures that confirm that God would radically answer your prayers if you, like Abraham, prayed for opportunities to do *tzedakah*:

"The LORD is far from the wicked, but He hears the prayer of the righteous." **Proverbs 15:29**

"Confess your trespasses tone another, and pray for one another, that you may be healed. The effective, fervent prayer of a righteous man avails much." **James 5:16**

THE KEY TO EFFECTIVE PRAYER

Combined, these two Scriptures give us a powerful master key to effective prayer in the Kingdom of God. The first thing we must understand is that God is more inclined to answer our prayers when we act as priests whose goal in prayer is that *others* would receive the goodness, generosity and kindness of the Almighty. The second thing we need to understand to be effective in prayer, is that God answers the prayers of those who consistently practice *tzedakah*. In other words, if you are a person who consistently seeks to be a blessing to others then God will seek to be a blessing to you (Genesis 12:2-3) and if you forgive others then you too will be forgiven. In Hebrew culture and language this concept is called *"midah kneged midah,"* which means "measure for measure" and is the principle that Yeshua was explaining in the following Scripture:

"Judge not, and you shall not be judged. Condemn not, and you shall not be condemned. Forgive, and you will be forgiven. Give, and it will be given to you: good measure, pressed down, shaken together, and running over will be put into your bosom. For with the same measure that you use, it will be measured back to you."
Luke 6:37-38

So what does it mean that "the same measure that you use, it will be measured back to you?" It means that God's response to you is measured by your response to others. When you show mercy or kindness to others, God will show kindness to you. When you give to others what they need when they are in need, then God will give you what you need, when in need. If you seek opportunities every day to be a blessing to others, then God will seek every day to bless you. And if you are an answer to others' prayers, then God will be the answer to your prayers. And if you seek to help others before they ask for your help, then God will answer you before you ask or even call on Him. This is the principle of *midah kneged midah* or measure for measure. It is the foundation for understanding why God says that He hears and answers the prayers of the righteous.

Two examples from Scripture where God hears and answers prayer on behalf of the righteous are found in the book of Acts. First is Dorcus, a woman who was "full of good works and charitable deeds," who was restored to life because of her tzedakah (Acts 9:36-42). Second, is Cornelius who was "a devout man and one who feared God with all his household, who gave alms (gifts to the poor- tzedakah) generously, and prayed to God always." To him an angel appeared during the hour of prayer and explained that his prayers and alms (tzedakah) have come up for a memorial before God and he was heard because of his tzedakah (Acts 10:1-4, 31, 34-35).

Peter also summarized the importance of this concept of tzedakah in relation to our prayers being received by God in the following verse. *"Then Peter opened his mouth and said: In truth I perceive that God shows not partiality. But in every nation whoever fears Him and works righteousness is accepted by Him."* **Acts 10:34-35**

ABRAHAM RUNNING FROM GOD

Usually, when you hear talk about someone running from God, it is because of their own selfish reasons and ideas. For example, there are many people who have walked away from the church and their faith in God for many reasons. But that is not the type of running from God Abraham did although he did run from the presence of God. What I am about to share with you has been one of the most eye opening revelations I have ever received. And interestingly it has made me want to run from God also. So let's look at Genesis 18 to see what made Abraham run from God.

> *"Then the LORD appeared to him by the terebinth trees of Mamre, as he was sitting in the tent door in the heat of the day."*
> **Genesis 18:1**

Wait, just a minute! Who starts a sentence off with the word "then"? If someone approaches you and starts a conversation with the word "then", you are likely to be confused or misunderstand because you don't know what came before "then." The word "then" is an adverb that can be used in place of the phrase "at that time". So when our Scripture here in Genesis 18 starts out with "then," it's really saying, "at that time."

Now please forgive me, my intention is not to give you a grammar lesson, but if the word "then" is being used in the place of "at that time", we ought to ask the question, "At what time?" Or simply, "During what time period did the LORD appear to Abraham?"

This is one of the many cases where in reading Scripture if we are not careful we'll allow the chapter divisions to keep us from seeing the big picture. That's why we need to read the entire context of Scripture. For instance, for the current Scripture we are examining, we must understand what happened before Genesis 18:1, in order to truly understand what happened after Genesis 18:1. So let's go back a few verses in Genesis chapter 17 to get a better understanding of what's going on.

"'This is my covenant which you shall keep, between me and you and your descendants after you: Every male child among you shall be circumcised; and you shall be circumcised in the flesh of your foreskins, and it shall be a sign of the covenant between Me and you...'

Then He finished talking with him, and God went up from Abraham. So Abraham took Ishmael his son, all who were born in his house and all who were bought with money, every male among the men of Abraham's house, and circumcised the flesh of their foreskins that very same day, as God had said to him.

Abraham was ninety-nine years old when he was circumcised in the flesh of his foreskin. And Ishmael his son was thirteen years old when he was circumcised in the flesh of his foreskin. That very same day Abraham was circumcised, and his son Ishmael; and all the men of his house, born in the house or bought with money from a foreigner, were circumcised with him.

Then the LORD appeared to him by the terebinth trees of Mamre, as he was sitting in the tent door in the heat of the day. So he lifted his eyes and looked, and behold, three men were standing by him; and when he saw them, **he ran** from the tent door to meet them, and bowed himself to the ground, and said, My lord, if I have now found favor in Your sight, to not pass on by Your servant.

Please let a little water be brought, and wash your feet, and rest yourselves under the tree. And I will bring a morsel of bread, that you may refresh your hearts. After that you may pass by, inasmuch as you have come to your servant. They said, do as you have said. So **Abraham hurried** into the tent to Sarah and said, quickly, make ready three measures of fine meal; knead it and make cakes. And **Abraham ran** to the herd, took a tender and good calf, gave it to a young man, and he hastened to prepare it. So he took butter and

milk and the calf which he had prepared, and set it before them; and he stood by them under the tree as they ate.
Genesis 17:10 – 18:8, emphasis added.

LOOK TO BE A BLESSING EVEN WHILE YOU'RE IN PAIN

Do you see at what time period the LORD appeared to Abraham? It was just after he circumcised himself at 99 years old in obedience to God. According to Jewish teaching this divine visitation actually took place on the third day after his circumcision when Abraham would have been experiencing the most pain and discomfort.
But what is he doing in the doorway of his tent? And what does "in the heat of the day" mean?

Depending on where you live the heat of the day can be pretty hot. Considering the fact that Abraham was in the middle east in a desert area you'd have to think "heat of day" was a pretty hot time. The word used for heat of the day is from the Hebrew root word *"chamam,"* and it means "to be hot" or "to be enflamed." In other words, it is referring to the kind of heat that makes you feel like you're in an oven. It is also the kind of heat where people traveling on foot or on camels can become dehydrated quickly. In midsummer it is not uncommon for a person in a desert climate to consume 2 to 2 ½ gallons of water a day. Usually when it is this hot, people stay away from windows or doorways where they are likely to be more exposed to the heat (especially if you don't have air conditioning). So the real question is, why Abraham sat in the doorway of his tent, nearest the scorching heat on the day he is in the most pain from a surgery three days earlier on a very sensitive area?

Generally, when someone is standing in the doorway they are awaiting or looking for something or someone; perhaps guests. However, let's not assume we can interpret this Scripture based on our own understanding. The word translated as "sitting" is the Hebrew word "**yashab**", which means to sit in ambush, or to lurk (which is to lie and wait in concealment)... **In other words, Abraham was not sitting casually in the doorway of his tent observing the land. He was sitting quietly in concealment waiting to ambush someone with blessings.**

This reminds me of a time a good friend invited me to their ranch in the hill country of Texas to hunt deer with a few other friends. I had been hunting many times before for smaller animals, but never deer or anything that large. We went out into the woods, early in the morning before the sunrise, and climbed a ladder into a deer blind to sit and wait for the deer. The blind was a small aluminum box about fifteen feet off the ground, with a small rectangular opening for us to look out of and watch the deer. The purpose of this blind was not only to hide us from the deer, in a place where we could see them but they could not see us, but it also helped to cover our scent so the deer would not know where we were. From this position, we could easily ambush the deer and they would never know what was coming. This is what Abraham was doing in the doorway of his tent in the heat of the day.

This is definitely consistent with the picture of *tzedakah* we discussed earlier, which is to crouch or lay in a stealth position waiting for an opportunity to spring forth and be a blessing to the weak or needy. Just like a lion will lie in ambush near a watering hole during the heat of the day waiting for an opportunity to pounce on an animal weakened by thirst, Abraham was lying in ambush during the heat of the day, waiting to spring up to be a blessing to someone. This is also why several times during this passage it mentions that Abraham ran or hurried. A lion sitting in ambush doesn't just get up and casually trot over to the animal it is hoping to catch and devour, but it springs forth with such great speed and intensity, that it often has to sit a long while to recover its strength before it can begin eating its prey. In the same way, Abraham did not casually go after people he wanted to bless, but even while in pain he still exerted his strength for an opportunity to do tzedakah. Even more note worthy than why he was sitting in the doorway, is knowing that he was sitting there in spite of the pain or discomfort he felt.

    If there was anyone who had an excuse to look to be served or to be on the receiving end of a blessing that day it was Abraham. He could have easily had one of the orphans, (or foster children) who viewed him as father, sit in the doorway and offer water and food to passersby. But Abraham would not be outdone when it came to being a blessing to others! Neither would he defer an opportunity to be a blessing to someone else, even if he was in pain from an operation. Now do you see why God choose Abraham? Or here is a more relevant question; do you look to be a blessing to others only when you feel like it? Or, are you someone who can put your feelings and pain aside to help someone else?

    Let me assure you, the best time to test your love and willingness to be a blessing to others is not when everything is going well and you are feeling well, but when everything seems to be a struggle and you're in pain. Listen, it's easy to give out of abundance, the true test is giving out of poverty or when you are in need yourself.

ABRAHAM'S TREE

"Then Abraham planted a tamarisk tree in Beersheba, and there called on the name of the LORD, the Everlasting God."
Genesis 21:33

Have you ever planted a tree? I am moved by the idea of planting something beneficial to the community which may be around for decades and even centuries after you are gone. There are over 305 mentions of the word "tree" or "trees" throughout the Scriptures, all with some significance and meaning. Nonetheless, I believe this particular mention of Abraham planting a tamarisk tree tops the list in importance and revelation. But before I explain the significance of this particular tree planting, you should first know the symbolic meaning of trees in the Kingdom of God.

In the Kingdom of God, trees are symbolic of the righteous, or those who practice *tzedakah*. How so? They provide shade from the intense heat of the sun's rays. They also provide food/fruit that nourishes the hungry and are a resource of materials for building shelter. Finally, trees are firm and upright and representative of those who support the community.

Psalm 1, certainly one of the more well-known Psalms, uses a simile to explain that those who delight in the torah (or teachings and instructions of God) and meditate upon it day and night, will be like trees that bring forth fruit in season. This Scripture uses a simile, which compares two unlike things as being similar or alike. But this is not the only Scripture that likens the righteous to trees. Isaiah 61 also uses this same imagery of the righteous being like trees:

"The Spirit of the LORD God is upon Me, because the LORD has anointed Me to preach good tidings to the poor; He has sent me to

heal the brokenhearted, to proclaim liberty to the captives, and the opening of the prison to those who are bound... That they may be called trees of righteousness, the planting of the LORD that He may be glorified. And they shall rebuild the old ruins, they shall raise up the former desolations, and they shall repair the ruined cities."
Isaiah 61:1-4

THE REPAIRING POWER OF TZEDAKAH

In this Scripture it is not only implied, but directly stated that the righteous shall be called "trees of righteousness" (verse 3). However, this Scripture in Isaiah 61 also gives us specific detail of some things those "trees of righteousness" were doing. The Scripture not only implies that the righteous were anointed to bring good news to the poor, heal the broken, deliver those in captivity and comfort the mourning, but it also says they rebuild the ruins and raise up former desolations. Now this is where it gets really interesting. The word for "ruins" is the Hebrew word *"chorbah,"* and it refers to the kind of desolation caused by drought and extreme heat. If you happen to live in an agrarian society in which crops are the main source of your economy and income, this type of desolation means economic desolation.

So what do the trees of righteousness do during economic desolation? They rebuild, which is the Hebrew word **"banah,"** which also means "to obtain children." This gives a very strong imagery that the righteous, not only seek to repair broken economies, but while they are working to help repair the ruined economy, they provide and care for those affected as if they were children of their own household.

I think we need to get a better understanding of the "former desolations" mentioned in Isaiah 61:4 and better understand the role of the righteous in such places. The word "desolation" in Isaiah 61:4 is **"shamem,"** and it refers to a place that appears to have been wasted or totally devastated. And the word translated former is **"rishon"**, which means first in place or rank. This gives the imagery of the places with the worst kind of deprivation and destitution, which are the kind of places that trees of righteousness are attracted to and the kind of places that we see ministries like World Vision, Feed the Children and Life Today campaigning and raising tzedakah for. It is the kind of place that the righteous work to make good, to raise up from the ashes, and to transform it into something beautiful.

CHAPTER 8 POWER POINTS

- Through Abraham we learn that rather than focusing on asking God to bless us, we should focus on asking God to enable us to be a blessing to others.
- As Abraham sat in ambush looking to be a blessing to others, we to should looking to ambush others with blessings.
- Tzedakah is the key to effective prayer, because God's response to us is measured by our response to others. As you through your kindness and generosity are an answer to others prayers, God will respond kindly and generously toward your prayers.

Chapter 9

YOU SHOULD LOOK LIKE A TREE

Do you remember earlier we discussed that according to the Hebrew method of study called *midrash*, you can study the Scripture on four different levels. The *peshat* (surface), the *rimez* (hint/allegory), the *drosh* (the application) and the *sod* (mysteries of the Kingdom). Well, I want to use that principle now to show you that being made in God's image means you should be like a tree.

The Hebrew word used for tree is **"etz,"** spelled with the letters *ayin* and *tzadi* (עץ). Well the *peshat* or surface meaning is in fact that a tree is... a tree. However, let's look below the surface by examining the numerical value of the word *"etz"* since every Hebrew letter is also a number. The numerical value of *ayin* is 70 and the numerical value of *tzadi* is 90. Together these add up to 160. Interestingly, according to the *midrash*, there is often great significance and meaning in words sharing the same numerical value. So what other word shares the same numerical value of 160 with the word *etz*? The Hebrew word *"tslem"* (צלם) is an example of one such word. The numerical value of *tzadi* is 90, the value of *lamed* is 30 and the value of *mem* is 40. Together these add up to 160, the same as the word *"etz"* for tree.

So what does the word *tslem* mean? It means **"image"** and is first used in Genesis 1:26 when God says "...Let us make man in our <u>image</u>, according to our likeness." What does this mean? The fact that the word for tree (*etz*) and the word *tslem* used for being made in God's image have the same numerical value, mean to teach us that man appears to be in God's image when he is like a tree

92

which is firm and upright. In other words, man looks like (the image of) God when he is doing tzedakah (righteousness). This also means that if you want to appear to others to be made in God's image, you must first appear to be like a tree to others.

YESHUA IS LIKE A TREE

If it is true that to be made in God's image is also symbolic of being like a tree, can we find any place in the Scripture where Yeshua, (God in the flesh) is compared to a tree? Yes, of course.

In Mark's account of the gospel, there was a blind man brought to Yeshua who saw something very interesting when he was in the process of receiving his sight. Take a look at the account below:

> *"So He took the blind man by the hand and led him out of the town. And when He had spit on his eyes and put His hands on him, He asked him if he saw anything. And he looked up and said, I see men like trees walking."* **Mark 8:23-24**

Wow! How peculiar that a tree is symbolic of the righteous and this man saw men in the appearance or image of trees. What does this mean? Well, the surface meaning is that his returning vision was blurred, but the deeper meaning is that He saw Yeshua and His disciples who were doing acts of *tzedakah* appearing in the image of God. This is consistent with the idea that mankind, when doing *tzedekah* or righteousness is both like a tree and like the image of God. So here's an interesting question to ask oneself; are you like a tree or a bush in your community? A tree, as we now know, represents a life of *tzedekah* or charity and generosity that helps to support a community. This is the kind of life that attracts and comforts others. The Hebrew word for bush is *"seneh"* and is a picture of a thorn bush, which actually causes people to change directions to avoid being pricked by its thorns.

BECOMING A TREE OF TZEDAKAH

In one of His parables on the Kingdom, Yeshua compares the Kingdom of Heaven to a mustard seed, which grows into a tree that provides a resting place and shelter for a variety of birds (Matthew 13:31-32). Through this parable one of the things we learn is that the Kingdom of Heaven is like small seeds that at first appear to be insignificant in stature, but grow to be the primary support for the community. Don't despise small beginnings!

ARE THERE ANY TREES IN YOUR COMMUNITY?

In the book of Numbers when the Children of Israel sent spies to search out and investigate the land to see what it was like, they were told to investigate several things:

- Are the people are strong or weak?
- Are they few or many?
- Is the land is good or bad?
- Is the land is rich or poor?

These are obvious things that one would want to know when moving to a new community. Nevertheless, they were also told to look for something that was pretty peculiar. They were told to investigate *whether there were any trees in the land or not* (Numbers 13:20).

Maybe this request does not sound strange to you. Maybe you're the type of person that investigates and searches for trees when you relocate to an area. We'll agree that the *peshat* of this Scripture is just as it sounds. They were to look for and examine the trees in the land of Canaan.

But now that we know that trees also have symbolic meaning is there possibly anything else that this search for trees could include besides physical trees? Of course! They were also searching the land for people who were firm and upright. For people who through *tzedakah* were the pillars of support for the community. For individuals who mirrored the image of God as trees of righteousness.

DON'T DESTROY THE TREES DURING WAR

I know now that you may be thinking about other places in the Scriptures where the mention of trees could also be more significant than you previously thought. Furthermore, I'm sure if you search for yourself you can find places where trees refer to more than just wood. For example, in the book of Deuteronomy God explains what to do with the trees of a land during warfare. Take a look at what He says below:

"When you besiege a city for a long time, while making war against it to take it, you shall not destroy its trees by wielding an ax against them; if you can eat of them, do not cut them down to use in the siege, for the tree of the field is man's food. Only the trees which you know are not trees for food you may destroy and cut down. To build siege works against the city that makes war with you, until it is subdued." **Deuteronomy 20:19-20**

On the surface, this Scripture is obviously instructing us not to cut down trees that may be used for food during war, but to use non-food-bearing trees to build armaments to assault the enemy.

But the deeper meaning is that even during war or redevelopment of a community, you must spare the righteous of the land. God's mindset is to spare both the trees that can be used for food and the righteous in a land. God saves the righteous and He will spare the land on the account of the righteous.

SODOM DESTROYED BECAUSE OF ITS LACK OF TREES

Traditionally, it has been taught that Sodom and Gomorrah were destroyed by God because of sodomy or homosexuality. However, although homosexuality is a sin and an abomination before God, the Scriptures do not say that Sodom and Gomorrah were destroyed because of homosexuality. God very clearly explain to us in the Scriptures why He chose to destroy Sodom and Gomorrah. To paraphrase it and put it in the context of this book, these cities were destroyed because they lacked trees. Yes, you read that correctly. Sodom and Gomorrah were destroyed because the land was deficient in trees. The land lacked people who were firm and upright. It lacked people who were trees of righteousness. Now I know that this may sound a bit different from what you have previously heard. But what did God tell Abraham he would need to find in order to spare the city? Read the biblical account of Abraham's intercession for Sodom:

"And Abraham came near and said, would You also destroy the righteous with the wicked? Suppose there were fifty righteous

within the city; would You also destroy the place and not spare it for the fifty righteous that were in it? Far be it from you to do such a thing as this, to slay the righteous with the wicked, so that the righteous should be as the wicked; far be it from You! Shall not the Judge of all the earth do right? So the LORD said, if I find in Sodom fifty righteous within the city, then I will spare all the place for their sakes..." Then he said, Let not the Lord be angry, and I will speak but once more: Suppose ten should be found there? And He said, I will not destroy it for the sake of ten." **Genesis 18:23-26, 32**

God told Abraham that He would spare Sodom if He found just 10 **righteous** people. Now, do you remember who the righteous are according to Scripture? He who practices righteousness or *tzedakah* is righteous or a *"tzadiyq"* (1 John 3:7). In other words, God promised Abraham that if He found just 10 people who practiced *tzedakah* and were like firm and upright pillars of support in Sodom, that He would spare the land. These are individuals who faithfully and firmly support the poor and needy in their community through pursuing justice and charitable giving. Christian teachers have taught that what God was looking for was for 10 people who were perfect or had a high degree of holiness. However, we can't argue with the text. God did not say if He found 10 *holy* people, he would spare it the city. He said if He found 10 *righteous* people. This is not to downgrade the importance of holiness in any way. It is still true that without holiness, no one will see the LORD (Hebrews 12:14). The point here is that God did not specify holiness as the prerequisite for sparing the city, but rather *tzedakah*.

THE SIN OF SODOM

We have discussed the demise of Sodom and Gomorrah as being the result of its lack in trees. Now let's look at how God explains the fall of these cities through the prophet Ezekiel, to see if there is any consistency or if we can confirm the idea of these cities being destroyed because they lacked trees of righteousness.

> "Look, this was the iniquity of your sister Sodom: She and her daughter had pride, fullness of food, and abundance of idleness; neither did she strengthen the hand of the poor and needy. And they were haughty and committed abomination before Me; therefore I took them away as I saw fit." **Ezekiel 16:49-50**

There are a few words used in this passage of Scripture that, when understood, give clear imagery to the cause of Sodom's end. The first is the Hebrew word used to refer to the iniquity of Sodom is *"avon,"* which means "perversity." The second word is the Hebrew word translated as "pride," which is *"goan"* and means arrogance or haughtiness. And the last word we should understand in this text is the Hebrew word for "idleness," which is the word *"shaqat"* and refers to doing nothing or not employing one's self or ones resources in a productive manner.

Now when you read Ezekiel in light of these words, you'll see that God explained that the worst perversion of Sodom was not homosexuality. The perversity that caused God to demolish Sodom, was the fact it was so arrogant and selfish that it would not even employ the abundant bread and resources it possessed to help the poor and the needy. In other words, Sodom was a city full of people who did not practice *tzedakah* and would not support the poor and needy of their own community. But let me bring this a little closer to home. God considers not doing *tzedakah* to help the poor and needy as a worse perversion than homosexuality. Again this does not mean that homosexuality is not a sin, because it is. However, isn't it interesting that in citing the reason for destroying Sodom,

God doesn't even mention homosexuality as the reason for its downfall?

Another question for you to consider: Many churches preach against homosexuality, fornication, lying, stealing, drunkenness and other transgressions of God's commandments, but shouldn't they preach just as much, if not more, about the importance of doing *tzedakah*? When asked, Yeshua indicated that the greatest commands were to love God with all your heart, and to love your neighbor like you love yourself.

My primary goal for you reading this book or hearing this teaching is not to teach you what not to do or what sins to avoid. Rather it is to teach you, or help you better understand, how to do what God wants us to do. That is, how to love your neighbor as *yourself,* which is primarily manifested through *tzedakah* and loving kindness.

THE NATURAL AND SPIRITUAL GEOGRAPHY OF SODOM

As you study the Scriptures you must keep in mind that many of the things that we read may hold deeper significance than we may realize. The method of study called *remez* uses identifying and examining things like names, numbers, dates, irregularities and repetitions in the Scriptures. Interestingly, as you read about Sodom in the Book of Genesis you'll discover that several times the Scriptures repeats a particular description of Sodom's Geography. Below are the verses below that each strangely repeat Sodom's geographic description:

"And Lot lifted his eyes and saw all the plain of Jordan, that it was well watered everywhere (before the LORD destroyed Sodom and

Gomorrah) like the garden of the LORD, like the land of Egypt as you go toward Zoar." **Genesis 13:10**

"So He overthrew those cities, all the plain, all the inhabitants of the cities, and what grew on the ground." **Genesis 19:25**

"Then he looked toward Sodom and Gomorrah, and toward all the land of the plain; and he saw, and behold, the smoke of the land which went up like the smoke of a furnace." **Genesis 19:28**

"And it came to pass, when God destroyed the cities of the plain, that God remembered Abraham, and sent Lot out of the midst of the overthrow, when He overthrew the cities in which Lot had dwelt." **Genesis 19:29**

Did you see the description that was repeated four times in each of the four verses above? It is the word **"PLAIN,"** which is repeated four times. Why did God feel the need to repeat the geographical description of Sodom four times? Is there any significance or relevance to Sodom being located in a plain area? Do you know what type of topography you find in a plains area?

A plain is a relatively flat landscape that is often referred to as grasslands, where the dominant type of vegetation is grass, herbs and other <u>NON- woody</u> types of plants. In other words, the plains are geographical areas that do not have many trees (or woody plants). The fact that Sodom was described geographically as a place located in a plain meant that it was also lacking in trees. Being that trees are symbolic of the righteous, do you think it is mere coincidence that God was also unable to find ten righteous individuals in Sodom? Probably not. Although, it does confirm the idea that God destroyed Sodom because it did not have enough trees (of righteousness). It also helps us to identify the location of the "Sodoms" of the world today, which are not necessarily communities where homosexuality is dominant, but areas that lack trees or people that are firm and upright, who support the poor and needy through *tzedakah*.

GOD SPARES A TREE IN SODOM

"Riches do not profit in the day of wrath, but righteousness delivers from death." **Proverbs 11:4**

Have you ever read or heard about the tree in Sodom, which God spared from the destruction of fire and brimstone that rained down on Sodom? No? Well, let me show you what I mean. We reviewed a Scripture earlier where God instructed His people not to destroy the trees of the land, especially the fruit trees (Deuteronomy 20:19-20). Then we read God's promise that He would not destroy the righteous with the wicked. Well, from the fact that God destroyed Sodom, but spared Lot, we can also conclude that Lot was a tree of righteousness in an area that was both spiritually and physically lacking in trees. Moreover, just as we were able to see in scripture that God destroyed Sodom because its people did not practice *tzedekah* (Ezekiel 16:49), we can also conclude that God spared Lot because he did practice *tzedekah*. Look at what the apostle Peter has to say about Lot's righteousness in the midst of Sodom:

"And turning the cities of Sodom and Gomorrah into ashes, condemned them to destruction, making them an example to those who afterward would live ungodly; and delivered righteous Lot, who was oppressed by the filthy conduct of the wicked for that righteous man, dwelling among them, tormented his righteous soul

from day to day by seeing and hearing their lawless deeds." **2 Peter 2:6-8**

Now that you have a Scripture that confirms that Lot was righteous, let's examine an instance of Lot practicing *tzedakah*. Please keep in mind that Lot was part of Abraham's household who, God said, teaches his household to follow after the ways of the LORD to do justice and *tzedakah* or righteousness (Genesis 18:19). This is our first insight into the potential of Lot's training in tzedakah. Then in Genesis 18:1 as we discussed earlier, we see Abraham sitting in the tent of his doorway, waiting in ambush to be a blessing to passersby. Now let's fast forward to Genesis 19 to see how Lot was following the example of His father (through adoption) Abraham.

> *"Now the two angels came to Sodom in the evening, and Lot was sitting in the gate of Sodom. When Lot saw them, he rose to meet them, and he bowed himself with his face toward the ground. And he said, here now my lords, please turn in to your servant's house and spend the night, and wash your feet; then you may rise early and go on your way. And they said, no, but we will spend the night in the open square. But he insisted strongly; so they turned in to him and entered his house. Then he made them a feast, and baked unleavened bread, and they ate."* **Genesis 19:1-3**

The Hebrew word used to describe how Lot sat in the gate of the city is the same Hebrew word *"yashab,"* which is used to describe how Abraham sat in ambush in the doorway of his tent looking for an opportunity to spring forth and be a blessing to the needy. It's no coincidence that Lot is repeating the behavior of Abraham recorded one chapter earlier. Being raised in the household of Abraham, Lot would have not only been trained to practice *tzedakah*, but he would have frequently seen Abraham seeking (opportunities to do) *tzedekah* (or righteousness).

There are a couple of words used in this passage, that when we examine them more closely will bring clarity to this event. The Scripture tells us that upon first meeting, Lot requested these angels, who appeared as men, be guests of his home for the night. They declined his offer. At this point we are told that Lot then insisted strongly that they accept his offer of hospitality. The word "insisted" is the Hebrew word ***"patsar,"*** which means to stubbornly peck at something until it becomes dull. The word translated as "greatly" is the Hebrew word ***"mehode,"*** which means to do something with intense feeling and exertion of energy. Together this gives the imagery that Lot was not just casually requesting that these strangers allow him the opportunity to do an act of tzedekah for them. But he continued to seek and request this opportunity to do tzedakah with such great intensity until he eventually wore them out. Just as a wood pecker continues to stubbornly peck at a tree until it creates a hole in the tree into which it can fit, Lot continued to peck at these men with his request that they allow him to give them comfort in his home until they could no longer refuse.

By the way the fact that the angels at first rejected Lot's hospitality was no coincidence, it was a test. If you remember, God told Abraham that He would **LOOK** (or search) for any righteous individuals living in Sodom before He would destroy it (Genesis 18:26). How do you look for or test someone's righteousness? Not by their church attendance or even their Bible study habits. To test a person's *tzedakah* you have to present them with an opportunity to do *tzedakah* and see how much they are willing to endure to do *tzedakah*.

This means that the angels rejecting Lot's initial offer of hospitality was actually a test of Lot's *tzedakah*. Why? Because righteousness is best tested when comfort and convenience to do *tzedakah* is absent. The truth of the matter, is we don't really know how long Lot continued to persistently petition these men to accept his offer of hospitality. It is very possible that he could have continued asking them for 45 minutes or more before they said yes. All we know for sure is that he kept insisting until he eventually wore them out and their "no" became a "yes." And for this reason the following scripture was written:

"And turning the cities of Sodom and Gomorrah into ashes, condemned them to destruction, making them an example to those who afterward would live ungodly; and delivered righteous Lot..."
2Peter 2:6-8

CHAPTER 9 POWER POINTS

- As trees often provide shelter, food, and shade from harsh conditions, they are symbolic of how we are to be as trees of righteousness in our communities.
- It is when we function as trees of righteousness that we most resemble the image of God.
- God saves and spares the righteous, but don't forget that He destroyed Sodom, because they refused to share their bread with the hungry.

CHAPTER 10
SEEKING TZEDAKAH AT ALL TIMES

"Blessed are those who keep justice, and he who does righteousness at all times!" **Psalm 106:3**

You may have read the parable in the Bible about the widow who continued to petition the unjust judge until she received justice, and the judge only answered to prevent her from wearying the him with her continuous requests for justice. Well, Lot gives us the example of not taking no for an answer, when it comes to your opportunities to be a blessing to others. In other words, resistance to an opportunity for him to do *tzedakah* was futile. Lot's example of *tzedakah* should cause each of us to examine how many times and for how long will you seek an opportunity to do an act of *tzedakah* for someone? Is one "no" or one minute of requesting your limit? Or are you like Abraham and Lot who were neither deterred by pain or a "no" from doing *tzedakah*?

Make no mistake about it. God wants you to pursue *tzedakah*, but not with a casual attitude, nor only when it is convenient. We are to pursue it like Abraham did. We should act as if our existence is prolonged and our life strengthened through doing *tzedakah*. This is what the psalmist has in mind in Psalm 106. Blessed and praiseworthy is the person who constantly looks to perform *tzedakah*. This is the type of person who most resembles the goodness of the image of God.

ABRAHAM'S SHELTER

"For you have been a shelter for me, a strong tower from the enemy." **Psalm 61:3**

Now, we will discuss the significance of the kind of tree Abraham planted in Genesis 21:33. I thought it was important for you to have a good understanding of the significance of trees in the Kingdom of God. In many ways trees support a community even by just sheltering people from the hostile rays of the sun.

In a related manner the psalmist in Psalm 61 also speaks of the LORD acting as a shelter from one's enemy. How is this Scripture related to Abraham's tree? The Hebrew word translated as enemy is *"oyeb,"* from a root word that means "to hate" or "to be hostile towards." In other words, in the same way that a tree shelters and protects people from the hostile rays of the sun, the Father shelters and protects us from a variety of things that are "hostile" towards our existence. Just like a tree, the righteous should seek to shelter others from various things that are "hostile" to the existence of others, regardless if the enemy is extreme heat or cold, hunger, thirst, sickness, poverty...you name it.

With this in mind you would probably be interested to know as we examine Abraham's tree that the Hebrew word used for the type of tree Abraham planted is not the word *"etz,"* which is the word most commonly translated as "tree." As a matter of fact, the word translated for the kind of tree planted by Abraham is only used three times in scripture, while the word *"etz"* for tree is found 287 times.

So what kind of peculiar tree did Abraham plant? The Hebrew word for Abraham's tree is ***"eshel"*** (אשל). This word *"eshel"* is a very peculiar word "from a root of uncertain meaning" according to some scholars. But an examination of the ancient Hebrew pictograph of the letters forming the word *"eshel"* can show us the meaning and image of what Abraham planted.

The *aleph* (א) is a picture of an ox and represents strength.

The *shin* (ש) is a picture of teeth and represents consuming, and the *lamed* (ל) is a picture of a staff or cattle goad used to move the cattle forward and represents the idea of walking, moving forward or journey. Together this gives the imagery of an *"eshel"* as a place where one can be strengthened, from consuming (eating and drinking) to continue their journey. Does this sound similar to any place in your community? Or is there any place in your community you can think of where people who are traveling can go to eat, drink and rest in order to be strengthened in order to continue their journey? How about a local hotel or lodging place? Well that's about the only thing that fits the description of an *eshel* in our day. Hence, Abraham's tree was a tree in the sense that it was a place that provided both shelter and food.

Remember I said that a number of Christian scholars view the word *"eshel"* as being from a root of uncertain meaning. Well the word *eshel* (אשל) is also an acronym for

(א)*achilah*, (ש) *shetivah* and (ל) *linah*. What does *achilah*, *shetivah* and *linah* mean? Eating (*achilah*), drinking (*shetivah*) and lodging overnight (*linah*). In other words, just as a tree provides a place for food, shelter and rest for the birds that travel the air ways,

Abraham's tree was a lodging place, or a place established to show hospitality to the community and wayfarers.

Is this just coincidence? Not likely, especially when you examine the context or events prior to Abraham building this lodging place. In case you don't remember, prior to the tree planting, Abraham makes a covenant with Abimelech and Phichol the commander of Abimelech's army, in which Abraham swore to continue to show kindness to their people and the land (Genesis 21:22-34). It is as a direct result of this promise or oath that Abraham made to show kindness to the people of this land, that he proceeds to plant a tamarisk tree indicative of his desire to carry out and fulfill his oath of kindness.

But wait because it gets better... After Abraham "built" this *eshel*, "He called on the name of the LORD, the Everlasting God" (Genesis 21:33). As we discussed earlier the word translated as "called" is *qara* and it means "to encounter" or "to invite guests." We already know that and yet it's still exciting to know that, through inviting people to be beneficiaries of our hospitality and kindness, we are also inviting the LORD.

Did you know that the Hebrew word translated as "Everlasting" God is **"olam"** which is from the Hebrew root word **"alam,"** which means "to veil or conceal from sight?" This gives us the understanding and imagery that through inviting and welcoming guest to a place that he had built specifically to show hospitality and kindness, Abraham was indirectly proclaiming the goodness and kindness of God. Wow! How liberating it is to know that we can teach others about the kindness of God, without directly mentioning His name, but by just being intentional about showing others the goodness and kindness, which God has shown us.

SEIZING THE MOMENT

Earlier I mention that Abraham ran from the presence of God (Genesis 17:26- 18:3). The LORD appeared to Abraham after his circumcision when he was sitting in ambush in the doorway of his tent. Suddenly, while in God's presence (at the doorway of his tent), he looks up and sees three men and runs speedily out of the doorway, **WHERE THE PRESENCE OF GOD WAS,** to invite three strangers into his tent to be refreshed with water and nourished with bread. Now I don't know what your belief or background is or what your thoughts are about having the opportunity to be in the presence of God, but here is an example of someone who preferred to give a glass of water to the thirsty, than sit in the blessedness of God's presence! Scripture describes being in the presence of God as a place of fullness of joy and perpetual pleasures (Psalm 16:11). Yet, in Genesis 18:1, when Abraham in significant pain had the chance to be a beneficiary of God's blessings, he chose instead to be a benefactor to the weak and needy. Now do you see why God choose Abraham? Now do you see why he was considered great amongst men? Most people are only focused on being a recipient of blessings, but Abraham would rather be a *distributor* of blessings. And scripture says is it more blessed to give than to receive (Acts 20:35)! Remember though, Abraham viewed his life, not as dependent on receiving blessings, but on dispensing blessings.

CHAPTER 10 POWER POINTS

• At all times and in every place we should look for opportunities to do tzedakah. This will cause God's blessing to look for you at all times and in all places.

• Abraham taught us that practicing tzedakah is the most effective way to teach the nations about the generosity and kindness of our God.

• Many religious people act as if building a house or edifice for God, is necessary for people to believe that God cares for them and that they should believe in Him. However, and contrary to popular religious thinking, it is when we build shelters for people that they believe God cares and are provoked to believe.

CHAPTER 11

INCREASING YOUR NOBILITY AND EQUITY IN THE KINGDOM OF GOD

"Now beyond all contradiction the lesser is blessed by the better."
Hebrews 7:7

There are some who teach that all people are viewed the same or have the same rank before God. Although God is no respecter of persons (Acts 10:34) he does regard one's efforts or contributions. Of course the Scripture says all of God's people are royalty, but don't be deceived, there is still ranking amongst the royal family of God. This scripture from Hebrews 7 gives us insight into how rank is determined in the Kingdom. It simply tells us that the lesser is blessed by the better. The word better is the Greek word *"**kreitton**"* and it means "stronger" and "nobler." In other words, the more we bless others, the more we increase our nobility and equity in the Kingdom of God. Wow! What an idea, that in the Kingdom of God your value or equity is not increased by accumulating goods or assets, but through distributing goods and serving others for their benefit.

Ok, now let's confirm this idea of increasing your nobility and equity in the Kingdom through serving others. In the gospel of Luke it is recorded that Yeshua's disciples had a discussion about which of them would be the greatest or noblest of His disciples. Read the account of this incident below:

"Now there was also a dispute among them, as to which of them should be considered the greatest. And He said to them, The

> *kings of the gentiles exercise lordship over them, and those who exercise authority over them are called benefactors. But not so among you, on the contrary, he who is greatest among you, let him be as the younger, and he who governs as he who serves. For who is greater, he who sits at the table, or he who serves? Is it not he who sits at the table? Yet I am among you as the One who serves."* **Luke 22:24-28**

Yeshua taught them that the greatest amongst the people of His Kingdom are the greatest servants. But there's more! The word translated as "serves" comes from the Greek root *"**diakonos**,"* from which we get the word "deacon." That is very interesting and fairly contrary to common ideas about who the greatest people are in the Kingdom of God.

I mean, Yeshua just said that the greatest in His Kingdom are the deacons. Really? Not the apostles, prophets, evangelists, pastors or teachers? Now before you mistake this as me interpreting this as saying that a deacon is the greatest title, I am not. Every title, whether apostle, prophet, or pastor is just that a title. As such these titles are really only labels that identify a particular function. That means when Yeshua says the greatest among you is the "deacon," he was saying the greatest among you is the one who fulfills the function of a deacon. In other words, whatever the function of a deacon is the kind of work that receives the highest honor in the Kingdom of God. So what does it really mean to be a deacon? Or better yet, what is the function of a deacon?

The Greek word for "deacon" is actually derived from the Hebrew word ***gabbai tzidekah*** *(pronounced "se- diq-ah")*. So what is a *gabbai tzidekah*? A collector of *tzedakah* (or charity collector). This means that a deacon, in the original sense, was someone who actively sought after *tzedakah* or charity to help the poor and needy. They would often go door to door with something called a *tzedakah* box to collect *tzedakah* or charitable donations to help those in need. As a matter of fact, this was initially the responsibility of those appointed in Acts 6:1-7. They were in charge of daily collection and distribution of *tzedakah* to the widows. Now here is an interesting question: How many of these types of deacons do you have at your church? Who in your church or community is in charge of collecting and distributing *tzedakah* to those in need in your church or community?

THE STARS OF THE KINGDOM

"Those who are wise shall shine like the brightness of the firmament, and those who turn many to righteousness like the stars forever and ever." **Daniel 12:3**

If your desire is to be significant in the eyes of God, strive to be a deacon or a *gabbai tzidekah* to be exact, which again is a person who seeks to both raise awareness of the needs of others and seeks to raise charitable contributions to be distributed to the needy. Having been in and around the ministry for years I am aware of how common it is to hear someone say they have been called by God to preach, teach or pastor. Others say they are called to be an evangelist, prophet or apostle. But only on rare occasions, do I remember someone saying that they have been called to serve. Likewise, I don't know if I have ever heard someone say they believe God is calling them to function as a deacon or collector or *gabbai tzidakah*.

Yet, if the greatest and most honorable function in the Kingdom is to collect and distribute charity for the needy, then why do people not seem to hear God's call to serve in this capacity? You have probably heard people talking about the how great a preacher is at delivering an awesome and encouraging word, but have you ever heard anyone discuss how great someone is for raising an offering for the needy? Or how great someone is for making sure the poor or needy are taken care of? Perhaps this is because our priorities are not always in line with God's thoughts and priorities. In the twelfth chapter of Daniel we are given more insight into the identity and work of those who are the "stars" or "celebrities" in the Kingdom. Not celebrities in terms of TV personalities or people well liked by many. Rather, a celebrity in terms of someone who is celebrated as someone significant or highly honored in the Kingdom of God because of their work and contributions. So let's take a look at this Scripture and then analyze it closer.

"Those who are wise shall shine like the brightness of the firmament, and those who turn many to righteousness like the stars forever and ever." **Daniel 12:3**

The first question we might ask about this scripture is: "Who are the "wise" spoken of here?" The Hebrew word translated here as "wise" is not the traditional or common word used to identify a wise person, *"chakam,"* but rather, *"sakal,"* which means "to have knowledge and understanding of how to instruct others." As a matter of fact, this word is used in the eleventh chapter of Daniel specifically to speak of those who have the ability and understanding of how to instruct others.

"And those of the people who understand shall instruct many..."
Daniel 11:33

As previously stated, the word translated "understand" is the same Hebrew word *"sakal,"* used here to speak of those who instruct others. That means this group of wise people spoken of in this Scripture are those who instruct God's people. It is said of these wise ones that they will shine like the brightness of the firmament. Firmament in Hebrew is ***"raqiya"*** and refers to the visible sky within the Earth's atmosphere, which is illuminated by the sun. That means the brilliance or light of the teachers is comparable to the light of the sky when it is brightened by the sun's light. To put it another way, this Scripture is teaching us that the reward of those who enlighten others is that they will also enlighten like the sun enlightens the day. This is an awesome reward for teaching others and helping them to understand God's Word.

But there is a still greater reward and a greater prize that will be received by others.

THE POWER TO TURN OTHERS TO RIGHTEOUSNESS

While it is obviously a great thing to teach people and help them to *understand* God's Word, it is greater to actually enable and empower them to *do* God's Word. This is the difference between these two groups spoken of in Daniel 12:3: one group instructs, while the other is actually said to cause people to turn to righteousness (*tzedakah).* What does it mean that they turned many to righteousness? It is to cause many people to give generously and commit to the practice and the performance of charitable deeds. This is the work and mission of the deacon or the *gabbai tzidekah* or charity collectors, to give people the opportunity to perform *tzedakah*. This also applies to the minister of the gospel who encourages people to give their tithes, offerings and other gifts for the work of the ministry. In essence, every time an individual, whether in ministry or not, encourages someone to give toward a need, they are giving that person or group the opportunity to perform *tzedekah* or righteousness. Even more interesting is that according to rabbinical interpretation of Scripture the individual who causes others to give *tzedakah* for a particular cause is actually partially credited for the benefit brought about by the measure of *tzedakah* they solicited. As a matter of fact, during biblical times beggars in Israel and other parts of the Middle East, when soliciting aide from passers by would not typically ask for money directly. Instead they would utter the words, "TZEDAKAH! TZEDAHAH!" Why? Because they were not just asking for a person to give, but to act in righteousness towards their cause.

Every time the deacons or charity collectors give people the opportunity give *tzedakah*, they give that person an opportunity to increase their equity and nobility in the Kingdom through the performance of *tzedakah*. In turn they also increase their own status in the Kingdom of God. Through Daniel 12:3 God explains that the merit or reward of the one who teaches is to be eternally enlightened like a cloudless day sky, which is illuminated by our local star called the sun. However, for those who cause many to practice *tzedakah*, they will shine like the actual stars themselves which illuminate the day sky. In other words, the brightness or glory of one who both pursues and teaches others to perform *tzedakah* will exceed that of the teacher of mere information.

This idea of the charity collector being more honored or receiving a greater reward is also confirmed by the prophet Isaiah in the following verse:

"The work of righteousness will be peace, and the effect of righteousness, quietness and assurance forever." **Isaiah 32:17**

While this is a good translation, the Hebrew translation of this verse does a better job of more clearly communicating the idea and the meaning this Scripture. Take a look at the difference:

> "And those who effectuate the performance of charity will have perfect peace, while the work of giving charity will cause everlasting tranquility and security." **Isaiah 32:17** (from the Orthodox Jewish Bible)

Interestingly this particular translation teaches that those who cause others to give charity will have perfect peace, while those actually give charity will have tranquility and security. To put it another way, those who simply perform *tzedakah* will be have secure rest, while those do *tzedakah* and cause others to do *tzedakah* also will have perfect peace, which means that they will have absolutely nothing lacking which would diminish their joy.

TEACHING OF A HIGHER ORDER

I have a background as an educator and I know that many teachers are trained to help students develop an ability to use higher order thinking skills. In order to accomplish this, educators employ a matrix that we use in lesson planning called Bloom's Taxonomy, which is a classification system for learning objectives. According to Bloom's there are six levels in the cognitive learning domain, which progressively require and demonstrate higher levels of learning. Here they are listed below with 1 being the lowest level and 6 being the highest level:

1. Knowledge
2. Comprehension,
3. Application,

4. Analysis

5. Evaluation

6. Synthesis (sometimes evaluation is considered the highest level).

The last 3 are considered the higher order thinking skills. Any teacher desiring to be effective in educating and equipping their students strives to incorporate these higher skills in lessons to ensure maximum level learning. The idea here is that we take learners beyond mere knowledge and comprehension of Scripture, to a level of mastery where they can synthesize or create entire communities that are saturated with the wisdom of Kingdom culture. Unfortunately, much of Christianity is content with followers simply comprehending the knowledge of Scripture, when our goal should be that believers are able to evaluate their environment and culture in light of Scripture and create the reality of the Kingdom within their own sphere of influence.

CHAPTER 11 POWER POINTS

- The more we bless others through our tzedekah the more we increase our nobility and equity in the Kingdom of God.
- The greatest and most esteemed in the Kingdom of God are the charity collectors, or those who raise awareness and resources to help the needy.
- Those who turn others to the practice of tzedakah will shine in the Kingdom like the stars forever and ever.

CHAPTER 12
THE MINISTRY OF MESSIAH

"But now He has obtained a more excellent ministry, inasmuch as He is also Mediator of a better covenant, which was established on better promises." **Hebrews 8:6**

It is interesting that one of the most important focuses of Yeshua's ministry is often the most overlooked. When we speak about Yeshua dying on the cross for our sins as only taking care of our spiritual shortcomings we actually miss the mark (again). The Scripture does not just teach that He died on the cross for our sins, but that *"He himself took our infirmities and bore our sicknesses."* (Matthew 8:17). The word used here for "infirmities" refers to "weaknesses" or someone "without strength." Obviously, this fits well within the definition of *tzedakah* as we discussed earlier, as it explains that Yeshua's ministry is to remove the weakness, not the weak. This also helps us to understand that Yeshua's ministry mission went well beyond the issue of sin. His mission was to minister to both the spiritual and physical conditions of mankind. This is an important point to note, because traditional teaching says that salvation is only a spiritual issue, and as a result, focus on ministering to the needs of the spiritual man. This is the type of doctrine that would cause someone to try and lead someone else to salvation and ignore their physical, mental and emotional state.

Please do not be deceived into thinking that this was how Yeshua operated in bringing salvation to the world. As a matter of fact, look at what the apostle John had to say about the person who tries to minister only to the spiritual needs of man:

> "By this we know love, because He laid down His life for us. And we also ought to lay down our lives for the brethren. But whoever has this world's goods, and sees his brother in need, and shuts up his heart from him, how does the love of God abide in him? My little children, let us not love in word or in tongue, but in deed and in truth." **1 John 3:16-18**

In other words, Yeshua did not just verbalize the love of God in some abstract intangible form, but He actually made the love of God evident to us, by his concrete actions and deeds. The message does not just stop there, the apostle John clears up any doubt or confusion about how we also demonstrate God's love and it is not only through communicating the message of salvation. Leading someone who is starving, in the sinner's prayer (as a first response to their overall condition) is not how we demonstrate God's love. The way to demonstrate God's love to someone who is starving is to *feed them!* The way to demonstrate God's love to someone who is thirsty is to give them something to drink. The way to demonstrate God's love to someone who is sick is to visit them. This is what the apostle John is trying to teach us in asking: how is it evident that God's love is in us when we do not respond to people's physical needs?

HOW PROFITABLE IS FAITH WITHOUT GOOD WORKS?

Thankfully Apostle John isn't the only one to bear witness to this truth regarding how we illustrate God's love. Look at what James says about the true evidence of our faith:

"What does it profit my brethren, if someone says he has faith, but does not have works? Can faith save him? If a brother or sister is naked and destitute of daily food, and one of you says to them, Depart in peace, be warmed and filled, but you do not give them the things which are needed for the body, what does it profit? Thus also faith by itself, if it does not have works is dead." **James 3:14-17**

It isn't a coincidence that when James teaches that it is our *works* that validates and gives true evidence of our faith, that he uses an example of being spiritually minded and praying for the physical needs of others without addressing the needs of the body. I love the question he asks about this kind of ministry, which is: **How profitable is it to only minister to the spiritual needs of a person or a community?**

Wow! What a question to ask spiritual people! What kind of return or harvest does one get when you're only ministering to the spiritual needs? And how does that compare to the profitability of one who ministers to both the spiritual and physical needs of others? Clearly, James is of the opinion and belief that ministers and churches would be much more profitable and productive to have a faith which ministers equally to both the spiritual and physical needs of people.

I believe that we, who are attempting to follow Christ, would greatly benefit by heeding the words of James and John. We must seek to follow the example of Yeshua. Even Yeshua Himself, when asked by John the Baptist for proof that He was the Messiah who was to come did not respond by the commenting on the things He was preaching or teaching. Instead, He reminded John of the things *He was doing*. In other words, He focused on the good works that He was doing to minister, not only to the spiritual, but even more so to the physical needs of the people. Take a look for yourself at what Yeshua said validated that He was in fact, the Coming One:

"And when John had heard in prison about the works of Christ, he sent two of his disciples and said to Him, are You the Coming One, or do we look for another? Jesus answered and said to them, Go and tell John the things which you hear and see: The blind see and the lame walk; the lepers are cleansed and the deaf hear; the dead are raised up and the poor have the gospel preached to them."
Matthew 11:2-5

Wow! How interesting that Yeshua's proof of His being the Messiah was His good works towards those in need. This is not the only place that Yeshua points towards His good works as evidence of who He is. Take a look at what He says during the Feast of Dedication, also known as Chanukah, when a group of Jews cornered Him to ask plainly if He was the Messiah:

"Then the Jews surrounded Him and said to Him, how long do You keep us in doubt? If you are the Christ, tell us plainly. Jesus answered them, I told you, and you do not believe. The works that I do in My Father's name, they bear witness of Me... I and My Father are one. Then the Jews took up stones again to stone Him. Jesus answered them, Many good works I have shown you from My Father. For which of those works do you stone Me?... If I do not do the works of my Father do not believe Me: but if I do, though you do not believe Me, believe the works, that you may know and believe that the Father is in Me, and I in Him." **John 10:24-38**

THE GOOD WORKS OF TZEDAKAH

Again here in the previous passage we see Yeshua pointing towards his good works as the greatest evidence that He is the Messiah. What are good works? And how does one define them? The Hebrew word translated as "good" is *"tov,"* and means "something that is good because it is functional or that it functions properly." This helps us to understand that good works are the kind of works or labor which results in something functioning properly. It also is the idea of work that enables or assists with a particular function. So in the beginning when God said that what He had created was good, He was proclaiming that what He had created was functioning properly.

In the Hebrew language, when something is not functioning properly it is called *"ra,"* which means evil. For example, when a person is dehydrated from thirst or malnourished from hunger their physical body will begin to malfunction or become *ra* (evil). However, when you labor to provide water or food to someone, you enable that person's body to continue to function properly. In other words, by your good works you have not only increased the good in the world by enabling someone to function correctly, but you have also diminished the evil (*ra*) by eliminating a malfunction.

Can you imagine how the world would look if God's people were just as zealous about eliminating the evils or malfunctions caused by hunger, thirst, poverty, broken heartedness, etc., as they are about other things they consider to be more spiritual? Isaiah prophesies that the end result of such activity would be a group referred to as "trees of righteousness" and the planting of the LORD (Isaiah 61:3). In other words, these individuals would be identified and referred to as those who the LORD has planted or placed in their midst. In Hebrew this idea or concept of eliminating evils or malfunctions and repairing the functionality of the world is called *"tikkun olam"*, which means "repairing the world." To be sure, this was the work of Yeshua and is the work of His followers – *tikkun olam*, to repair and rebuild, to continue working to make things good (properly functional).

By the way, did you notice that Yeshua explained that the works He was doing were also the works of the Father (John 5:19-21; 10:32)? Do you remember what the works of the Father are? The work of the Father is to do the work of a tent-pole. In other words, the work of the Father is to lift the household or family (of mankind) out of the dirt and lowly positions. It is to strengthen the weak and to sustain the poor and needy; to do justice and *tzedakah* (Jeremiah 22:15-16).

This means that when Yeshua pointed towards His good works to validate His ministry He was in fact highlighting His *tzedakah* as the chief witness of who He claimed to be. So much so that He even excuses people who do not believe the things He says are true just because He said it. This is no small statement. Here you have Yeshua, the Messiah, God in the flesh saying that He will not hold you accountable if you don't believe what He says, just because He says it... Think about that! If Yeshua pointed towards His *tzedakah* as proof that He was the Messiah, why do you tell people that you know He is the Messiah (if you do)? Furthermore, **If Yeshua taught that His works of tzedakah validated who He said He is, then what do you tell others validates that you are a follower of His?**

THE WORKS OF CHRIST

Let's review some of the works Yeshua did to make the lives of others more functional (also known as "good works"). For starters, consider the time Peter's mother-in-law was bed ridden with a fever. Obviously, the fact that she is bed ridden means she is not as functional as normal. However, with just a touch from Yeshua, her fever left and she arose and served them, which means she returned to normal function. (Matthew 8:14-17)69
How about the time they brought a man to Yeshua who was paralyzed? Yeshua then healed and returned his body's muscular and nervous system functions back to normal (Matthew 9:2-7). Or how about in Matthew 9:27-29 when two blind men called on Yeshua to restore the function of their eyes? Certainly, we could continue for quite some time recalling the times Yeshua made something or someone's life more functional. As a matter of fact, take a look at what Apostle John said about all the things Yeshua did:

"And there are also many other things that Jesus did, which if they were written one by one, I suppose that even the world itself could not contain the books that would be written. Amen." **John 21:25**

In Matthew 5:22, Yeshua indicates that anyone who calls his brother Raca, or worthless, is in danger of the council and anyone who calls his brother fool, or stupid, is in danger of hell fire. The point here that is consistent with this topic is that, if someone says that his brother is worthless rather than seeking to increase his brother's worth, he is in danger of being brought before the council. Furthermore, someone who goes beyond just calling his brother worthless, but says you are in fact too dumb or stupid to become worth more is in danger of hell's fire. How many times have you heard someone talk negatively about the men that sit on their porch drinking all day in the inner city or turn their nose up at the homeless? Interestingly, I have met homeless people with Ph.Ds and great ideas. As followers of Christ, our job is not to dismiss them as individuals with no value, but to identify the value within them and help to bring it out. By doing so, we not only improve their lives, but we improve the lives of the community at large. The more value we can bring out of our brother, the more value we add to our community and the more we increase our own equity in the Kingdom of God.

REAL INVESTING

Those familiar with real estate investments understand this concept. In real estate, the equity and worth of a house can be increased just because the surrounding home owners have done things to add value to their own homes. In the same way, when citizens of the Kingdom reach out to help and invest in their neighbors, by default they increase their own value and equity in the Kingdom of God.
 So let's not look at the young boy standing on the corner with his pants "sagging," waiting on someone to come by drugs, and declare that he is worthless. Let's see the entrepreneurial potential in this young man and help draw it out of him. He is most certainly *not* too dumb to learn and develop the skills that can cause him to be great.

CHAPTER 12 POWER POINTS

- Yeshua's ministry was not just to save us from our sins, but to deliver us from bondage, oppression, poverty, sickness and anything that diminished our existence as children of the Kingdom.
- It is both more profitable and productive to minister to both the spiritual and material needs of people than to only minister to the spiritual needs of others.
- Anyone who views or speaks of a person as worthless rather than seeking to increase that persons worth and esteem is in danger or hell's fire.

CHAPTER 13
SONS OF THE KINGDOM

"... You are the Christ, the Son of the living God." **Matthew 16:16**

I believe that we have clearly shown that what Yeshua said confirmed or validated Him as THE Savior and Messiah was His good works or *tzedakah*. In the same way we can also demonstrate that Yeshua was in fact the Son of God. In the biblical Hebrew language the word translated as "son" is ***"ben,"*** which means "builder" and the pictograph is of building a house or household. It is also a picture of continuing the household. This means that there are a couple of things that can cause someone to be considered a son in the Kingdom of God.

The first thing that causes one to be considered a son is to build or add to the household by bringing more children into the family, either by birth or adoption. Hmmm...this means that Yeshua's heritage was confirmed by the fact that He added more children or sons to the family of God. Take a look at what the following Scripture says about many children brought into the family of God because of Him:

"But as many as received Him, to them He gave the right to become children of God, to those who believe in His name, who were born, not of blood, nor of the will of the flesh, nor of the will of man, but of God." **John 1:12-13**

The previous Scripture is one that certainly confirms Yeshua's heritage through His bringing many into the family of God. As I mentioned earlier, there is another way in which this can be confirmed. Remember the biblical idea here is one who builds up the household or one who enables the household to continue. This also means that a person who takes care of and supports the family of man (and God) are also considered to be sons of God. Obviously, the continuation of a household can be stopped or hindered by things other than not reproducing or not having children. It can also be stopped, by sickness or disease, or by starvation caused by famine or extreme poverty. A household can be ended by divorce or violence such as war, etc...

So a person who helps a person or family to overcome poverty, or sickness or starvation so that they can continue living would also be considered sons of God. As a matter of fact, this is the idea behind the following Scripture: *"Blessed are the peacemakers, for they shall be called sons of God."* **Matthew 5:9**

SONS OF PEACE

"Blessed are the peacemakers, for they shall be called sons of God."
Matthew 5:9

In the Kingdom of God the word for "peace," is ***"shalom,"*** meaning "wholeness" or "completion." It is the state where nothing is missing or lacking to keep a person from being whole or complete. For example, if someone is sick they are not *shalom* or "at peace." Also if someone is impoverished, hungry or suffering from dehydration or thirst they are not *shalom*. So the work of a peace maker is simply to help make others *shalom* or whole. To put it another way, a peacemaker works to add what is missing or lacking from others lives that prevents them from being whole or *shalom*. Now obviously if you have read the gospel accounts, you know that Yeshua was indeed a peacemaker or that He made people *shalom*. Take a look at a couple examples below where Yeshua makes someone whole.

"And when the men of that place recognized Him, they sent into all that surrounding region, brought to Him all who were sick, and begged Him that they might only touch the hem of His garment, and as many as touched it were made perfectly well."
Matthew 14:34-36

"Then great multitudes came to Him, having with them the lame, blind, mute maimed and many others; and they laid them down at Jesus' feet, and He healed them. So the multitude marveled when they saw the mute speaking, and the blind seeing; and they glorified the God of Israel." **Matthew 15:30-31**
"And when He had looked around at them with anger, being grieved by the hardness of their hearts, He said to the man, stretch out your hand. And he stretched it out and his hand was restored as whole as the other." **Mark 3:5**

There are many other Scriptures that we can review where Yeshua is acting as Son of God because He is making others whole. However, I would like to show you how Yeshua taught His disciples that helping others to become shalom was the greatest of priorities. As a matter of fact, Yeshua even taught His disciples that making people whole was to take priority over preaching the gospel to someone. Now I realize that may come as a shock to some, so take a look for yourselves at how Yeshua instructed His followers to go and preach the gospel of the Kingdom:

"Then He said to them, the harvest truly is great, but the laborers are few; therefore pray the Lord of the harvest to send out laborers

into His harvest. Go your way; behold, I send you out as lambs among wolves. Carry neither money bag, knapsack, nor sandals; and greet no one along the road. But whatever house you enter, first say Peace to this house. And if a son of peace is there, your peace will rest on it; if not, it will return to you." **Luke 10:2-6**

THE PRIORITY OF PEACE

Did you see that? Yeshua instructed His disciples whom He sent to preach the Kingdom to **first** say "peace" when they entered a house, even before they did anything else including preach the gospel. What did Yeshua mean by greeting a household with "peace?" Was it just a way of letting those you encounter know you come in peace without any ill intentions? Well it helps, of course, to understand the word for peace, *shalom*, which we discussed earlier. However, understanding the significance of a greeting in Hebrew culture makes this passage more transparent. In Hebrew culture, during the times of Yeshua and even among some Jews today it is customary to greet others with peace by saying *"shalom."* However, if the greeting was more formal they would say **"Shalom Aleichem,"** which means, "How is your peace?" In other words, this greeting of *shalom* was not just a statement, but also a question of, "How is your wholeness? Is there anything you are lacking to keep you from completion or wholeness?" So the idea of greeting someone with peace was not to let them know that you come peacefully, or without any ideas of harm or ill intent, but to communicate that you have come *to bring them shalom* or to help them attain a state of wholeness!

Unfortunately, so many followers of Christ miss the importance of *first* seeking to help people become whole physically, mentally, emotionally or economically, *before* helping someone become whole spiritually. What a great mistake to think that we can effectively win souls, by only focusing on the spiritual lack in people's lives!

Think about it! Don't you think people will be more inclined to believe that you represent a God who is concerned about their spiritual well being, if you demonstrate that He is also concerned about their physical well being? Do you think it is easier to convince someone of God's love for their souls if there is no love shown for their physical bodies? Now don't get me wrong, there will always be those you can convince of anything. However, as we discussed earlier, you can't really compare the fruitfulness and effectiveness of a ministry that serves the physical <u>and</u> spiritual needs of mankind, with one that only serves the spiritual needs.

To illustrate this let's take a look at a Scripture that is often referred to when speaking of the significance of winning souls.

"The fruit of righteousness is a tree of life, and he who wins souls is wise." **Proverbs 11:30**

Usually when you hear people quote this verse they only quote the part that says "he who wins souls is wise." Yet, that is not how this Scripture starts. It starts with "The fruit of righteousness (*tzedakah*) is a tree of life." This means that the effective soul winner doesn't just start with winning souls by teaching or preaching, but he or she starts with acts of *tzedakah*. This is what Yeshua taught His disciples when He sent them out to preach the gospel and win souls to the Kingdom. He taught them to first seek righteousness or opportunities to do *tzedakah*, to make others physically and emotionally whole. Then they can preach the gospel and win another soul.

SONS OF GOD

"For the earnest expectation of the creation eagerly waits for the revealing of the sons of God." **Romans 8:19**

Now does this mean you are responsible for fixing everyone's problems or for helping everyone to be made whole? No. However, it does mean that you should not just be a person who only talks about others' problems, but that you should be someone who at the very least discusses and works towards identifying solutions to others' problems. Maybe you don't have $15,000 to dig a well to provide clean water to a village of a 1500 people, but maybe you could encourage 1500 people to give $10 towards the well (or 150 people to give $100). Perhaps you don't have the knowledge or experience of how to counsel a couple facing a divorce, but maybe you can call around and help them find a qualified counselor. Even if you don't have the money to help a father financially support his family, you may be able to help him find a job or start a business.

So now when you read the Scripture that says all of creation is waiting for the revealing or manifestation of the sons of God, you know that this Scripture is not saying that the world is waiting for more people to simply profess God as their Father. Professing God as your Father is not what makes it evident that you are a son of God, but being one who helps make the world *shalom* or whole, does (Matthew 5:9). That is what all of creation is waiting eagerly for. That means that it is not your knowledge of Scripture or your attendance at religious events that causes others to call you a son of God, but through working to make others *shalom*, that they **will** call you a son of God.

THE KINGDOM BAR MITZVAH

"When I was a child, I spoke as a child, I understood as a child, I thought as a child; but when I became a man, I put away childish things." **1 Corinthians 13:11**

Some cultures have certain ceremonies, rites of passage or celebrations held for those who are transitioning into adulthood. These are events that mark one as now having adult responsibilities, especially the duty to work as an adult. In the Hebrew culture, this celebration is called a "***bar mitzvah***" for boys or "***bat mitzvah***" for girls. The words, for *bar* or *bat mitzvah*, simply mean son or daughter of the commandments. The celebration is a time when a son or daughter becomes legally responsible and liable for following the commandments of God. It is also a time to recognize the responsibilities of adulthood, and also the time that a son takes up the work or trade of his father. This ceremony or event usually takes place at around age twelve or thirteen for both genders. Thereafter, a son would also be identified with his father by his father's trade or work.

If your father was a fisherman then you would be a fisherman. Yeshua found James and John in a boat <u>with</u> their father, mending their fishing nets (Matthew 4:21). If your father was a carpenter, then it would be expected that you would also do carpentry work. This is why several times in the Scriptures the people do not just ask if Yeshua is Joseph's son, but they asked is He not the carpenter's son (Matthew 13:55; Mark 6:3). In other words, they were really asking, what is Yeshua doing teaching as a rabbi in the synagogue, isn't He supposed to be a carpenter? Yeshua is not a carpenter's son, He is the son of God, which means that as a son of God, He would do the work of His Father (John 5:19).

At what point does Yeshua acknowledge that He would do the work of His Father? Can we find Yeshua's *bar mitzvah* in Scripture? In Luke 2, we find Yeshua, at the age of twelve, sitting in the temple in the midst of the teachers astonishing them with His answers and then proclaiming that He must be about His Father's business (Luke 2:41-50).

THE SEED OF ABRAHAM

"They answered and said to Him, Abraham is our father. Jesus said to them, if you were Abraham's children, you would do the works of Abraham." **John 8:39**

As we discuss the idea or concept of being a child of God, we must understand that what causes us to be recognized as a child of God is not that we look like our Father. It is not a physical resemblance in form that we need, but a *physical resemblance in function*. In other words, we are sons because we are about our Father's (*Ab*) business of *tzedakah*. Our Father functions like a tent-pole, which lifts the tent out of the dirt and carries the burden of its weight. Therefore, as sons we do what we see the Father doing and by lifting others up, taking care of the household of man, and working to help make others whole (*shalom*) we are identified as sons of God.

"And if you are Christ's, then you are Abraham's seed, and heirs according to the promise." **Galatians 3:29**

In recent years there has been much teaching about the identification of followers of Christ as the seed of Abraham. The idea of being the seed of Abraham encompasses multitudes of the promises of God, even being heir to the world (Romans 4:13).

However, you don't just come to be recognized as a child of Abraham because of what you profess, or because you simply say the sinner's prayer. In the gospel of John, Yeshua explained to a group who called themselves the offspring of Abraham, that if they were really Abraham's seed then they would do the works of Abraham (John 8:39). If you remember we already discussed the fact that Abraham's work was the work of *tzedakah*. As a matter of fact, God Himself confirms that the children or the household of Abraham would be taught to do *tzedakah* (righteousness) and justice (Genesis 18:19). So please do not be deceived. It is not your lineage or your belief alone that publicly validates you as the seed of Abraham, but the fact that you do the good works of Abraham, which is *tzedakah*, that confirms your faith and heritage.

CHAPTER 13 POWER POINTS

- A true son or child of God is defined as one who builds up and up holds the family of God.
- Yeshua taught His disciples that identifying and addressing issues that hindered people from being whole, took priority over actually teaching about the Kingdom of God.
- It is not our preaching or knowledge of scripture that validates us as the seed of Abraham, but our good works of tzedakah.

CHAPTER 14
HOW TO CARRY YOUR CROSS

It is not only a good idea that we seek to make others *shalom* (whole) through our *tzedakah* (acts of righteousness), but Yeshua actually taught that it was a required mindset in order to truly follow Him. Where can you find that stated as a prerequisite to following Yeshua? Take a look for yourselves:

> "Then Jesus said to His disciples, if anyone desires to come after Me, let him deny himself, take up his cross, and follow Me."
> **Matthew 16:24**

> "Then He said to them all, if anyone desires to come after Me, let him deny himself, and take up his cross daily and follow Me."
> **Luke 9:23**

> "And he who does not take his cross and follow after Me is not worthy of Me." **Matthew 10:38**

In all three of the previous Scriptures we have Yeshua teaching that if we desire to follow Him or be His disciples that we must *first* take up our own cross. Traditionally, people have taught that carrying your cross is the idea of being (figuratively) crucified and hated by the world. I have heard many Christians refer to this Scripture when discussing how others don't like them because they are Christian. Although Yeshua was indeed crucified on the cross, representing a place of suffering, this is not what He means when He says that His followers must also take up their cross before following Him. So what does the cross mean or represent? What was the principal idea of the cross? It isn't enough just to identify the cross as a place of suffering, but you need to understand the reason behind the sufferings of the cross. So here is what the Scripture says about the purpose behind the sufferings of the cross:

"who Himself bore our sins in His own body on the tree, that we, having died to sins, might live for righteousness – by whose stripes you were healed." **1 Peter 2:24**

"He Himself took our infirmities and bore our sicknesses." **Matthew 8:17**

Do you understand? The cross is symbolic of the suffering that Yeshua was willing to endure to carry the weight of our sins and iniquities. It was also symbolic of how he carried or shouldered the burdens of our sicknesses, diseases and weaknesses. It represented Yeshua taking care of a debt that we could not repay and carrying a burden for us that we could not carry. This means that the idea of taking up your cross is to have the same mindset to bear one another's burdens even if it means we have to sacrifice or suffer a little while (Galatians 6:2). To put it another way, for you to take up your cross daily means to be willing to put someone else on your back and help shoulder the weight of their burdens. This is also what the apostle Peter was trying to communicate through the following Scripture:

"Therefore, since Christ suffered for us in the flesh, arm yourselves also with the same mind, for he who has suffered in the flesh has ceased from sin," **1 Peter 4:1**

Let me try and paraphrase to you what Apostle Peter is saying in the previous Scripture: "Since Christ willingly and physically suffered to help carry you through your own short comings (sins) and weaknesses (infirmities), then we who claim to follow His life and example should also have the mind to willingly carry others' burdens."

YESHUA AS SAVIOR

"I have waited for your salvation, O LORD!" **Genesis 49:18**

It is very important that as followers of the Messiah that we have a more holistic understanding of salvation. Many times we have heard the message of salvation as a message about how Yeshua died on the cross for our sins and was raised from the dead after three days, so that we can go to Heaven after we die. Is that all salvation is? Is it just about the work that God has done to make your next life great? Let me say that I don't believe that there is anything that is more important to the well being of your spirit, soul and body than this great salvation given through Yeshua. With that in mind, I also believe that it is important that we study and understand it fully. So let's at least get started.

The scripture in Genesis 49 is the first actual mention of the word "salvation" found in the Bible. The Hebrew word used here for "salvation" is, "**Yeshua**" (which is the name of the Savior or Messiah). This word *Yeshua*, means salvation and deliverance and comes from the Hebrew root word *"yasha"* which means to set free, to defend, to preserve and to rescue. Contrary to how it is often presented, the word and idea of salvation does not just refer to God's plan to deliver and rescue mankind from sin and death. It applies to *any situation* where one may need deliverance, freedom, protection or help with preservation. Someone can be saved from sin (obviously a spiritual issue), but a person can also be saved (*yasha*) from sickness, famine, poverty and even slavery.

Our first example of salvation in Scripture, where we actually find the second mention of the word salvation (*Yeshua*) is in Exodus 14:13, where the Children of Israel are being delivered (*yasha*) from bondage and slavery in Egypt. By the way the Hebrew word for Egypt is "**mitsrayim**" and is from the Hebrew root "**matsor**," which means "limitations" or "to hem something in." So Egypt does not just represent a physical place, but it represents a state or condition where one is suffering from limitations and oppression. Egypt is the idea of having severe limits placed on your life and potential, whether they be from sickness, famine, debt, poverty, etc. So here we have a first example of "salvation," (*Yeshua*) a group of people being delivered from limitations and bondage of an oppressive government.

We must see salvation as something bigger than a spiritual issue, if the world is to be truly transformed by the gospel. We must simply embrace the idea of Yeshua as representing deliverance and rescue from both spiritual and physical opposition.

A NEW PICTURE OF SALVATION

Hopefully you now have a more solid understanding of salvation or Yeshua as we have defined it all the way down to its Hebrew root meaning. Nevertheless, just in case you want, or need, a little more detail, let me explain what the Hebrew pictograph of the word for salvation. As we discussed earlier, the Hebrew root of *Yeshua* is

Yasha spelled with the following Hebrew letters (יֹשַׁע). The *yod* (י)

is a picture of the hand and represents work. The *shin* (שׁ) is a picture of teeth and is a picture of consuming, destroying or destroyer. And the *ayin* (ע) is a picture of an eye and represents watching. Combined this mean that **Yeshua (and or salvation) is a picture of one working as a destroyer watcher (or one working to watch for the destroyer).**

WHAT DOES A DESTROYER WATCHER LOOK LIKE

Can you think of any biblical examples of someone whose work or occupation fit the description of a destroyer watcher? Consider David, who as a shepherd watched over his father's sheep and defended them from potential destroyers, such as bears or lions (1 Samuel 17:34-36). This means that the picture of Yeshua's function is not only as a shepherd of God's people (John 10:11-16), but that He actively watches for things that could potential destroy any of His flock, and then He destroys the potential destroyers. It does not matter if the potential destroyer is sickness, famine, poverty or sin. Therefore the Scriptures says *"for this purpose the Son of God was manifested, that He might destroy the works of the devil."* (1 John 3:8)

So here is an interesting thought and then a question. We who believe on Yeshua are supposed to be followers of His life and example, right? So if Yeshua functioned as a destroyer watcher, then shouldn't those who follow Him watch over their neighbors for potential destroyers and work to destroy potential destroyers? Furthermore, if His ministry work was to deliver and rescue people from potential destroyers, then shouldn't we also seek to rescue people from potential destroyers? If your answer to those questions is yes, then you would be acting as Yeshua, following His example to begin identifying the things that could be or already are destroying those in your family and community, and then annihilate those things.

AN ANOINTING TO DESTROY THE DESTROYER

While there are many believers and ministers of the gospel who proclaim to be anointed by God to preach, I believe that the anointing has a greater purpose than preaching. Take a look at what Isaiah says an individual under the anointing will do:

> "It shall come to pass in that day that his burden will be taken away from your shoulder, and his yoke from your neck and the yoke will be destroyed because of the anointing oil."
> **Isaiah 10:27**

Simply put the prophet God says, through the prophet, Isaiah, that a person under the anointing will remove burdens and destroy the yokes that cause people to be weighed down and in bondage. So we don't have to be religious about defining the anointing within the context of pastors or evangelists or ministers of the gospel. Technically, if an individual's work is to remove heavy burdens and destroy yokes of bondage and oppression from the lives of others, they fit the description of one who is anointed. As a matter of fact, God even says there are some in government who act as His ministers to execute justice (Romans 13:1-6).

YESHUA AND HIS DISCIPLES WERE GABBAI TZIDEKAH

"Jesus said to him, If you want to be perfect, go, sell what you have and give to the poor, and you will have treasure in heaven; and come follow me." **Matthew 19:21**

Earlier we discussed the fact that Yeshua taught that the greatest in His Kingdom would be the *gabbai tzidekah* or charity collectors. Again these are individuals whose work or function is to raise awareness and support, i.e. *tzedakah,* for the poor and the needy. However, Yeshua did not just teach by word only, He also taught by example. That means that He didn't just *tell* His disciples the significance of being a *gabbai tzidekah* and not function in this role Himself, especially since He had such great disdain for hypocrisy. As a matter of fact, after explaining that the one who functioned as a deacon (*gabbai tzidekah*) would be the greatest in the Kingdom, He stated that He also functioned as a *gabbai tzidekah* (Luke 22:24-27). Take a look at what He says:

"For who is greater, he who sits at the table, or he who serves? Is it not the who sits at the table? Yet I am among you as the One who serves." **Luke 22:27**

The Greek word Yeshua uses to identify Himself as one who "serves" is the same word we discussed earlier *"diakoneo"* from which we get our word "deacon," and it is from the Hebrew word *"gabbai tzidekah,"* which is a collector of tzedakah, or charity collector. So in essence we have Yeshua explaining that the greatest in the Kingdom are those who function as *gabbai tzidekah* and that He Himself also was a *gabbai tzidekah* or charity collector.

THE COLLECTION TOOL OF TZEDAKAH

If it is true that Yeshua Himself functioned as a charity collector, then the obvious question we should ask is: "Where else do the Scriptures directly say or imply that He did so?" Before I point out where the scriptures allude to the idea of Yeshua being a collector and distributer of charity (or a *gabbai tzidekah*) it would help if you understood what a *gabbai tzidekah* used to collect *tzedakah* (or money given for charity). They used and carried a "tzedakah box," which was usually a small wooden box into which donations of *tzedakah* were placed.

Now that we've identified a very important tool used by the *gabbai tzidekah* to collect money given for charity, I think you will more easily see that Yeshua was a *gabbai tzidekah* after you read the following Scriptures:

"But one of His disciples, Judas Iscariot, Simon's son, would betray Him, said, why was this fragrant oil not sold for three hundred denari and given to the poor? This he said, not that he cared for the poor, but because he was a thief, and had the money box and he used to take what was put in it." **John 12:4-6**

"Now after the piece of bread, Satan entered him, then Jesus said to him, what you do, do quickly. But no one at the table knew for what reason He said this to him. For some thought, because Judas had the money box, that Jesus had said to him, buy those things we need for the feast, or that he should give something to the poor."
John 13:27-29

Both Scriptures above mention that Yeshua and His disciples had a money box. As a matter of fact, these are the only two Scriptures in the four gospel accounts where this word "money box" is found. Now obviously, this is no regular box used to carry money, but without some additional cultural knowledge of the times you could very easily read over it without realizing the implications of Yeshua and His disciples carrying this peculiar money box. So what is this peculiar money box they possessed? It is a *tzedakah* box, which was carried by *gabbai tizdekah* and many rabbis during the time of Yeshua (and still today) to collect *tzedakah* for the poor and needy. There are a few more clues that this money box is actually a *tzedakah* box and that Yeshua operated as a *gabbai tzidekah*, other than the fact that this box is called a money box. One clue is found in the first Scripture, John 12:1-8, where Judas specifically mentions that the very expensive fragrant oil could have been sold and the money given to the poor. Then, we are told that the reason that he made such a suggestion was not because he really cared for the poor, but because he was in charge of carrying the *tzedakah* (money) box and because he was a thief and would steal some of the money collected for *tzedakah*.

The next clue is found in the second passage mentioned above (John 13:21-29), where the disciples thought Yeshua was telling Judas to quickly go out give something to the poor because he had the *tzedakah* (money) box. Both these Scriptures clearly give the idea that Yeshua and His disciples were also *gabbai tzedakah* who collected *tzedakah* or money to give to the poor and needy. There are also other things that are recorded in the gospels that allude to the idea that Yeshua and His disciples were *gabbai tzidekah* and would help take care of the poor and needy. One example is the account of Yeshua feeding the five thousand with two fish and five loaves of bread. Usually when you hear someone discuss this, the focus is on the miracle of God's provision, but there was important conversation before the miracle that give us insight into how Yeshua and His disciples operated. Take a look at the conversation of how they would feed the multitude before Yeshua performed the miracle.

> "Then Jesus lifted up Hs eyes, and seeing a great multitude coming toward Him, He said to Philip, where shall we buy bread, that these may eat? But this He said to test him, for He Himself knew what He would do. Philip answered Him, two hundred denari worth of bread is not sufficient for them, that every one of them may have a little." **John 6:5-7**

> "But He answered them, you give them something to eat. And they said to Him, shall we go and buy two hundred denarii worth of bread and give them something to eat?" **Mark 6:37**

In the accounts of Yeshua feeding the five thousand above, we see that before Yeshua made the bread and fish multiply, He first told the disciples that they should feed the people. So in response to this command to feed the people they began to estimate how much it would cost to do so, which was probably more than they had (especially since Judas was in charge of carrying the *tzedakah* box).

There are a couple of things I would like to point out here. The first, is that usually we focus on how Yeshua did a miracle, but we may miss the fact that God only steps in to perform a miracle, where it is needed. In other words, if they had what they needed in their tzedakah box there would have been no need for the miracle in this particular instance.

The second point is that it was very common thing for Yeshua to naturally feed the poor and the needy by natural means (of buying food). This again is the work of the collectors of *tzedakah*, to collect *tzedakah* and then distribute it to the poor and needy. As a matter of fact, we actually have record of Yeshua saying that some of the people were following Him because of the physical food they were eating and not the spiritual bread He provided (John 6:26-27, 32-35).

DISTRIBUTION OF TZEDAKAH

"As it is written: He has dispersed abroad, He has given to the poor; His righteousness endures forever." **2 Corinthians 9:9**

Earlier, we discussed that even though there has been some difficulty in translating and understanding the full meaning of *tzedakah*, that one of the best words that one could use to translate the idea of *tzedakah* is charity. So many places in the Scripture where you find the word righteousness, you could also translate it as charity. As a matter of fact, the Scripture above is an example of a Scripture where righteousness (*tzedakah*) could be rendered as charity. When you read it with the idea of charity in mind instead of the word righteousness, you'll see that this scripture is referring to one who charitably distributes goods and resources to the poor and needy.

The biblical or Hebrew word used to describe someone who gives *tzedakah* or gives charitably to the poor and needy is a **"tzaddik"**, which we translate as righteous and is the origin of the word "saint". So, scripturally, one who does righteousness (or *tzedakah*) is called righteous (*tzaddik* or a saint). However, do you know a more modern term or word used to describe a person who consistently gives charity today? A **PHILANTHROPIST,** which is a compound of the word *"philos,"* which means "loving" and the word *"anthropos,"* which means "human being" or "humanity."

Combined, these mean that **philanthropy is "the love of humanity"**. Wow!

This makes sense, especially when you remember that the Hebrew word for love is *"ahav,"* which means to give. This also confirms the idea that we show love to humanity by giving charitably to humanity or by giving *tzedakah*. It also means that we can call a person who does *tzedakah* (i.e. righteousness) a philanthropist, one who loves humanity (and shows love to humanity).

Have you ever thought of Yeshua and His disciples as philanthropists? Interesting right? Well, maybe a more interesting thought is understanding that both *tzedakah* and philanthropy are the same idea, and Yeshua instructed His followers to pursue *tzedakah* or righteousness (Matthew 6:33). This means that Yeshua was also instructing His followers to pursue opportunities to do philanthropy.

YESHUA THE PHILANTHROPIST

I realize that it is different to think of Yeshua as a philanthropist, but the more you think about what He did, the more the image of Him as a Savior Philanthropist will settle in your mind. Especially after reading Scriptures, like John 3:16, "... for God so loved the world that He gave..." Or the Scripture where Yeshua tells a young man who wants to follow Him (and His example) to first sell what had and give to the poor (Matthew 19:21). There is a scripture in particular, that when we examine it more closely, will help us to clearly see that our Savior was a Philanthropist. It is also a Scripture that is pretty popular with charismatic believers and it describes what Yeshua did under the anointing. Take a look:

> *"How God anointed Jesus of Nazareth with the Holy Spirit and with power, who went about doing good and healing all who were oppressed by the devil, for God was with Him."*
> **Acts 10:38**

We already discussed earlier that the anointing destroys yokes and removes heavy burdens from people's lives, but I ask that you keep what the anointing does in mind as we discuss the main idea of this Scripture. Yeshua "went about doing good." While it would probably be sufficient to know that we would be following His example by just "doing good," it isn't good enough to "probably" be right. So before we define this word, which was translated as "doing good", let's examine what we already know from this Scripture. First, we know that He was anointed, which means that His work was destroying yokes and removing burdens from people's lives (Isaiah 10:27).

The second thing we know is that He healed those who were oppressed by the devil. The word translated here as "healed" means "to make whole" and carries the same idea as a peacemaker or one who works to make others *shalom* (Matthew 5:9). With that in mind, let's now examine this word translated as "doing good," which is the Greek word *"euergeteo,"* which means "**to be philanthropic**." So there you have it! God anointed Yeshua to make people whole through philanthropy!

So now let those of us who desire to follow Yeshua ask ourselves, "Are you following His example of removing others burdens and making them whole through your philanthropy?"

CHAPTER 14 POWER POINTS

• Taking up your cross, means being willing to shoulder and carry other peoples burdens and weaknesses as Yeshua carried yours.

• As followers of Yeshua, the Good Shepherd we are to diligently watch for and defending against things that could potentially destroy our neighbors.

• Yeshua and His disciples were philanthropist who went about doing good. This means that if desire to follow Yeshua we must also labor to heal and deliver others through our charity and generosity.

CHAPTER 15
THE PURPOSE OF THE GOSPEL

"For the Kingdom of God is not in word but in power."
1 Corinthians 4:20

The essence and purpose of the gospel is not to be preached, it is to become reality and to be made manifest. That means it is just not enough for ministers of the gospel to have a scholarly understanding of the Scriptures. This is why Apostle Paul said the following:

"And my speech and preaching were not with persuasive words of human wisdom, but in demonstration of the Spirit and of power, that your faith should not be in the wisdom of men but in the power of God." **1 Corinthians 2:4-5**

Here we have Paul, certainly a chief apostle, explaining that what made His ministry significant or effective was *not* the wisdom with which he taught, but in *demonstrating* the things he taught by the Spirit. The word translated here as "demonstration" here is the Greek word ***"apodeixis,"*** which means "to manifest" or "make something clearly evident." This means that Paul's mission was to not to preach the gospel only, but to make it evident or a reality to the people he preached to.

So how do we make the gospel of the Kingdom a reality? Well, we can start by defining the word gospel. Obviously, this is knowledge we must have if we will be successful at making the gospel a reality. The Hebrew word for gospel is "**besorah**" (בְּשׂוֹרָה),

which means to publish good news. Remember the Hebrew idea of something being good means that it is functional or that it works properly. The word "publish" means "to make something public." Together these help us to understand that the gospel is the idea of making something publicly functional. It also implies the main idea of preaching the gospel of the Kingdom is not about lecturing or preaching to others about the Kingdom of God. Instead, it is to make the functionality of Kingdom life evident to the public. **So for a church or ministry this means that if it is not public knowledge that they are making people and their community more functional, then they are not fully publishing the good news of the Kingdom.**

THE GOSPEL LIVES IN YOU AND THROUGH YOU

> *"... For indeed, the Kingdom of God is within you."* **Luke 17:21**

The gospel is not supposed to be confined to books or mere words that we preach, but the gospel should reside in flesh and blood. In other words, the gospel of the Kingdom should live through you. This is also what I believe the Luke had in mind when said, "the Kingdom of God is within you" (Luke 17:21). As a matter of fact, before he made that statement He explained that we would not even see the Kingdom of God by looking for it outside of those who are carriers of the Kingdom (Luke 17:20-21).

For those of you who are believers and followers of the Messiah Yeshua, there is more potential in you than you have ever imagined. Inside of you there is something that is growing and has the power to make your community and world function on a higher level. It is the Kingdom of God. So since the Kingdom of God is within you, what does it mean? What are you asking when you pray to the Father that His Kingdom come (Matthew 6:9-10)? Interesting question right? The Greek word translated as "come" is *"erchomai,"* meaning "to come," "to grow," "to appear," or "to increase." So, when you pray "Thy Kingdom come," you are in fact asking the Father to bring out of you the reality and potential of the Kingdom (you are carrying) to make Earth function more like Heaven.

THE GOSPEL MADE INTO FLESH

"In the beginning was the Word, and the Word was with God, and the Word was God… And the Word became flesh and dwelt among us, and we beheld His glory, the glory as of the only begotten of the Father, full of grace and truth." **John 1:1,14**

This passage of Scripture is very familiar to believers, which helps us understand that God did not just send the gospel of the Kingdom in word only, but He sent it in the Flesh. Have you ever examined the Hebrew word for "flesh?" If you haven't or it's been a while, let me show you something that you may not have seen or heard before.

The Hebrew word for "flesh" is *"basar"* (בשר)… Hmmm… Does that word look or sound familiar? Well it should, because it is actually the same as the Hebrew word for "gospel," which means "to publish good news."

How interesting that the word for gospel, which means to publish good news, is the same as the word for the flesh we live in! Basar… What does this mean? What is God trying to teach us? While I believe that there are many things we can learn from this, I'll just share a couple. The first is that God did not just "make" you, He published you like a book. You are God's Word made flesh, not THE WORD as in, His Son, but the "<u>w</u>ord" as in His other sons (John

1:12-14). I also believe this is part of the idea behind the following Scripture:

> *"You are our epistle written in our hearts, known and read by all men. Clearly you are an epistle of Christ, ministered by us, written not with ink but by the Spirit of the living God, not on tablets of stone but on tables of flesh, that is of the heart."*
> **2 Corinthians 3:2-3**

YOU ARE A GOSPEL PUBLICATION

> *"But even if our gospel is veiled, it is veiled to those who are perishing."* **2 Corinthians 4:3**

The second thing I believe we can, and should learn from the fact that the word for flesh and the word for gospel are the same, is that *you* are the gospel. Or to put it another way, you are good news! However, there is more insight here to understanding how the gospel is to be published. Namely, that God cannot publish the good news of the Kingdom without flesh. Why? The *besorah* (or gospel) only becomes good news or functionally good, when it is made into *basar* (or flesh). Take a look at what the prophet Isaiah said about those who publish the gospel:

> *"How beautiful upon the mountains are the feet of him who brings good news, who proclaims peace, who brings glad tidings of good things, who proclaims salvation, who says to Zion Your God reigns!"*
> **Isaiah 52:7**

Our job as followers of Yeshua, is to **be** the good news to our family, neighbors and communities, to labor to make the earth function more like Heaven. We are to make our neighbors and communities *shalom*; to be a destroyer watcher, who defends our family, neighbors and communities from potential destroyers. We must diligently seek opportunities to do *tzedakah* and elevate our world through our own philanthropic efforts. For housed in you is a Kingdom so powerful in goodness that you *must* publish it, and you only do so through your *tzedekah*.

Chapter 15 Power Points

- The objective of preaching the gospel of the Kingdom is to empower individuals and communities to function on Earth as though they were from Heaven.
- We should not focus our energies on preaching the gospel of the Kingdom as much as on being the gospel of the Kingdom.
- God's strategy for promotion and publicity of His Kingdom is through inspiring and leading you to do tzedakah.

CHAPTER 16

THE MASTER KEY TO THE KINGDOM

"LORD, who may abide in Your tabernacle? Who may dwell in Your holy hill? He who walks uprightly and works righteousness, and speaks the truth in his heart." **Psalm 15:1-2**

There has been much said about the keys to the Kingdom of God in recent years as the message of the Kingdom has re-emerged. Obviously "keys" are significant in that they enable you to lock doors and prevent entrance into a house. But they also allow you to unlock doors and be granted access into a house or specifically the household of God. Keys are symbolic of our level of access in the earth. In the same way, I believe that the "keys of the Kingdom" represent our level of access in the Kingdom of God.

As I have studied *tzedakah*, I have come to believe that *tzedakah* is in fact the master key for access into the Kingdom of God. By this I believe that it is the Key to opening a multitude of doors in the Kingdom of God. Now that you have a better understanding of *tzedakah,* let me show you a few of the Scriptures where the reference is made to the importance of righteousness for accessing the Kingdom of God.

"For I say to you that unless your righteousness exceeds the righteousness of the scribes and Pharisees, you will by no means enter the Kingdom of Heaven." **Matthew 5:20**

"If you know that He is righteous, you know that everyone who practices righteousness is born of Him." **1 John 2:29**

"And in every nation whoever fears Him and works righteousness is accepted by Him."
Acts 10:35

"LORD, who may abide in Your tabernacle? Who may dwell in Your holy hill? He who walks uprightly and works righteousness, and speaks the truth in his heart." **Psalm 15:1-2**

There are many more scriptures that we could examine on the importance of *tzedakah* to entering the household or family of God, but let's just take a look at one last Scripture from Psalm 15. Obviously, this a very important question asked by David, "LORD who may abide in Your tabernacle?" (Psalm 15:1). The word translated here as "tabernacle," is "tent" and is a reference to both the tabernacle and the house of God.

As we have discussed the significance and importance of *tzedakah* hopefully, we see that it is the key to entering the family of Abraham. According to Psalm 15 those who walk uprightly and work righteousness are able to enter the tent and household of God. Let me give you an example of how someone entered the tent or house of Abraham because of their uprightness and *tzedakah*.

SEEKING A QUALIFIED BRIDE FOR ISAAC

One of the most interesting stories in the book of Genesis is when Eliezar is instructed by Abraham to go and find a wife for his son Isaac. What makes this interesting is that Eliezar is not given instructions on what to look for in a wife for Isaac, one who was heir to the world and the promises of God. However, being raised in the household of Abraham, who God said taught his household to do justice and *tzedakah*, he would have been looking for a woman with characteristics and values that were in line with the household of Abraham (Genesis 18:19).

As he journeys looking for a wife for Isaac, Elieazar stops to pray to the God of Abraham to aid him in finding a wife for Isaac. Take a look at his prayer for the kind of woman He wanted God to help him find for Isaac.

"Then he said, O LORD God of my master Abraham, please give me success this day and show kindness to my master Abraham. Behold, I here I stand by the well of water, and the daughters of the men of the city are coming out to draw water. Now let it be that the young woman to whom I say, please let down your pitcher that I may drink, and she says , drink and I will also give your camels a drink – let her be the one You have appointed for Your servant Isaac. And by this I will know that You have shown kindness to my master.' And it happened, before he had finished speaking, that behold Rebekah, who was born to Bethuel, son of Milcah, the wife of Nahor, Abraham's brother, came out with her pitcher on her shoulder… And the servant ran to meet her and said, please let me drink a little water from your pitcher. So she said, drink my lord. Then she quickly let her pitcher down to her hand, and gave him a drink. And when she had finished giving him a drink, she said I will draw water for your camels also, until they have finished drinking. Then she quickly emptied her pitcher into the trough, ran back to the well to draw water, and drew for all his camels." **Genesis 24: 12-20**

In essence, Eleazar asks God to help him find a wife for Isaac who would not only be kind enough to offer water to a complete stranger, but would be kind enough to provide water for His ten camels. Now I'm not sure on how much you know about camels, but one camel can drink as much as 40 gallons of water at one time.

Since Eleazar had ten camels, Rebekah could have drawn over 400 gallons of water. It is certainly kind and an act of *tzedakah* to offer water to a complete stranger, especially when you have to draw it out of a well! Moreover, the willingness to volunteer to draw an extra 400 gallons of water for a stranger's camels is certainly an act of kindness! Do you realize how long it could have taken her to complete such a task? Maybe as much as several hours. This is what makes this so amazing; that Eleazar essentially asked the LORD to help him find a wife for Isaac, who was willing to spend several hours drawing as much as 400 gallons of water out of a well for a complete stranger.

Eleazar understood the wisdom in what King Solomon would state many years after he is gone: a truly righteous person would not only care for people, but will also regard and care for the life of his animals as well (Proverbs 12:10). Later, King Solomon also informs us that the virtuous woman would not only be one who speaks words of kindness, but one who also stretches out her hand to the poor and needy (Proverbs 31:20, 26). This is the kind of person that God searches for throughout the earth to add to the family of Abraham. Interestingly, did you realize that Abraham, Isaac, Jacob, Moses and even David were all shepherds. What does tending to animals as an occupation have to do with being chosen to lead God's people? Certainly, individuals who are kind enough care for and protect animals with their very lives are surely caring and loving enough to lead God's people.

HIS WIFE HAS MADE HERSELF READY

"... for the marriage of the Lamb has come, and His wife has made herself ready. And to her it was granted to be arrayed in fine linen,

clean and bright, for the fine linen is the righteous acts of the saints." **Revelation 19:7-8**

My hope and inspiration for writing this book is to see the fulfillment of this Revelation scripture. To help the wife or bride of Christ get dressed and ready for the marriage of the Lamb. For those of us who believe the Scriptures, we believe that Yeshua is going to return for a glorious church who is also His wife (Ephesians 5: 23-27). However, we must understand that Yeshua is not returning for a fiancé, but for one fully ready and qualified to be His wife. So what does it mean or what does it take to be the wife of Yeshua?

One of the ways that we can better understand what it takes to be the wife of Christ is by examining the first wife, who is Adam's wife Eve and the mother of us all. Interestingly, when God decides to make Eve as a wife for Adam He doesn't say I will make Adam a wife. Instead He says,

"I will make him a helper comparable to him." **Genesis 2:18**

Normally, when a person thinks of a bride or wife, what comes to mind is what a bride looks like, instead of thinking of what a wife does, or what the function of a wife is. Yet, when God introduces us to the first wife, He doesn't introduce her by form, but by function. So what is the function of a wife or a bride?

There are two words here we need to examine to better understand the wife of Adam and therefore the wife of the second Adam. The first is the word translated as helper, which is the Hebrew word *"ezer,"* which means "help" or "aid." This gives us the idea that a wife is someone who helps or aids the man in his work or mission.

The second word we need to examine to better understand the role of the wife is the Hebrew word translated as "comparable to him", which is the word *"neged,"* which means "opposite" or "counterpart." Together these two words give the idea that a wife is one who helps her husband with his work or mission by doing a part that is corresponding or complementary to his work. This also means that the wife of Christ is one who helps Him complete His work, by working in a corresponding and complementary manner. Since we already know and have discussed that the work of the Messiah is to do *tzedakah* (righteousness), then it makes sense that the Scripture tells us that the wife of the Messiah makes herself ready by getting fully dressed in fine white linen, which represents the idea that she is dressed to do the work of *tzedakah* (Revelation 19:7-8).

In essence the wife of Christ (Messiah) has the most beautiful working relationship with her husband. She is committed to doing the work that complements and that corresponds to His work. In other words, since Christ's work is both natural and spiritual, she does the natural *tzedakah*, and He does the supernatural *tzedakah* (also known as the righteousness of God). Let me give you a few examples of how this relationship works:

- She feeds the hungry bread from earth and He feeds them bread from Heaven.
- She gives the thirsty drink from earth and He gives the thirsty living water.
- She visits the sick and He heals them.
- She gives of her earthly wealth to the poor and He gives them treasures of Heaven.
- She visits those imprisoned and in bondage and He frees or delivers them.

- She gives *tzedakah* from Earth and He gives *tzedakah* from Heaven.
- She does the natural and He does the supernatural.

So if you will be the help meet of the Messiah, then you will be one who helps Him complete His work of *TZEDAKAH*. This is the meaning of Revelation 19: 7-8, of how the wife of the Lamb makes herself ready for the marriage. And if you will be a follower of Messiah, then you will follow His example of *tzedakah*. And if you will be a true believer in Messiah, then you will truly believe in His teaching and instructions to seek every opportunity to practice Remembering that all Scripture, every inspired word was written so that *you* would be fully equipped to be a worker of *tzedakah!* (2Timothy 3:16)

This is the master key to the Kingdom, which Yeshua has given us. He has shown us that *tzedakah* is the key to cultivating the culture of the Kingdom of Heaven on earth. It is the Key to eliminating what we call evil or dysfunction. It is the Key to destroying the yoke of bondage and releasing the blessings of Heaven over our families, business, governments and communities. However, we should not be content with only striving to be more righteous ourselves, for this is not the vision of the Kingdom. The vision of the Kingdom of God is summed up by the prophet Isaiah in the following verse:

"Also your people shall all be righteous; They shall inherit the land forever, the branch of My planting, the work of My hands, that I may be glorified." **Isaiah 60:21**

That ALL of God's people would be righteous, this is the desire of God. That the citizens of His Kingdom would not be known to other people and nations by their religious attendance or even their knowledge of scripture, but by their generosity and kindness. This is how the Father wants to be glorified through you. That others may see your good works and as a result glorify your Father in Heaven (Matthew 5:16). However, we must understand that this type of culture of tzedakah or righteousness will not just happen because we believe and wait on the return of the Messiah Yeshua. No, this manifestation of the Kingdom will not come because we wait and watch (Luke 17:20-21). Instead the Kingdom culture of tzedekah is a seed that we must each sow daily in order to reap a harvest of righteousness in our sphere of influence. This is what the prophet Hosea had in mind when inspired to utter the following words:

"Sow for yourselves righteousness; Reap in mercy; Break up the fallow ground, for it is time to seek the LORD Till He comes and rains righteousness on you." **Hosea 10:12**

Now I understand that for most people this will indeed be a challenge to become the kind of person who consistently seeks to be a blessing to others on a daily basis. After all many people are seem to be struggling to meet their own needs and the needs of their families. To these people it may seem impossible to focus on being a blessing to others, but is it? Well to you maybe this is impossible to live in this manner, but to God, NOTHING is impossible. If you simply accept the desire and believe it is possible to be a blessing to others through God, He will not only supply your bread (necessities for life), but He will also provide you with seed to sow in righteousness. As a matter of fact, look at what the apostle Paul said when encouraging the church at Corinth to practice and pursue tzedakah:

"And God is able to make all grace abound toward you, that you, always having all sufficiency in all things, may have an abundance for every good work. As it is written:
He has dispersed abroad, he has given to the poor; His righteousness endures forever.
Now may He who supplies seed to the sower and bread for food, supply and multiply the seed you have sown and increase the fruits of your righteousness.
2 Corinthians 9: 8-11

Please understand that it is this type of righteousness consciousness more than anything else that will set you apart from the world and causes people to glorify God. It is righteousness or tzedakah that is the preeminent characteristic of Kingdom culture.

"Therefore do not worry, saying, 'What shall we eat? Or 'What shall we drink?' or 'What shall we wear?' For after all these things the Gentiles seek. For your heavenly Father knows that you need all these things. But seek first the Kingdom of God and His righteousness, and all these things shall be added to you."
Matthew 6:31-33

Chapter 16 Power Points

- Tzedakah is the Key experiencing greater access and opened doors in the Kingdom of God.
- God selects individuals who practice kindness and tzedakah for leadership and promotion in His Kingdom.
- The bride of the Messiah will make herself ready through tzedakah.

TAKE ACTION NOW!

In the following pages you will find tools to help you get started in your journey to impacting the world through TZEDAKAH!

Personal Tzedakah Action Plan

If you think you have been impacted by gaining a better understanding of tzedakah or righteousness and you believe that this was the way Yeshua and His disciples lived, then I want to encourage you to take the next step. For if all we do is hear the word and are not doers of the word what profit do we gain from Heaven. However, if we commit to disciplining ourselves to obey the word then blessings are released for us from Heaven. I believe that there is nothing that will make God's presence, power, and blessings more evident in your life than practicing tzedakah. As a matter of fact, the only scripture where God not only allows, but actually encourages us to test His ability to bless us, is a scripture that challenges us to give (tzedakah) so that food and provisions may be given from His house (Malachi 3:10-12).

God so desires His name and any house associated with His name to be known for generosity and kindness that He promises that if you unleash your tzedakah that He will unleash Heavens treasury of blessings in your life. Therefore regardless of your present level and practice of tzedakah, I invite you to take the Tzedakah Challenge over the next 31 days and personally experience the transformational work God will do within you, your community and sphere of influence as you release the ancient power of tzedakah.

Take a look at the 7 step Tzedakah challenge action plan on the next page and keep in mind that the overall the goal of the Tzedakah Challenge is that you would become more righteous (1John 3:17), and to attract the blessings of Heaven to you and your community.

7 Step Tzedakah Challenge Action Plan

1. Complete the tzedakah report card to examine your current practice of tzedakah. Ask God to forgive you for any selfishness and for not bringing glory to Him by being more of a blessing to others through tzedakah (1John 1:9).
2. Commit to functioning as a priest of the Kingdom for the next 30 days and only pray for the needs of others to be met that God may be glorified for His kindness and generosity (1Peter 2:5,9).
3. Ask God to show you opportunities to do tzedakah and supply you with resources and ideas (2Corinthians 9:8-10).
4. Identify needs where your generosity or *tzedakah* would make a difference (Psalm 112:5-9)
    a. in your immediate sphere of influence: family, friends neighbors, co-workers/ classmates, church family, etc.
    b. in your community: charities serving the community, schools, poor, widows, orphans
    c. in your state, nation, and world
5. Actively look for and seek opportunities to do at least one act tzedakah for someone else everyday for the next 30 days (Psalm 106:3; Matthew 6:33).
6. Record your acts of tzedakah in a journal and how you believe it made a difference to others.
7. Pray that God would turn others into practitioners of righteousness. Share the message of *tzedakah* or even this book with at least 3 other people (remember the significance of those who turn others to doers of righteousness). Gather a group of 2 or more people to start a Tzedakah group to make a difference in your community and bring glory to God.

Tzedakah Report Card

Read each statement below. Using the following numbers, score yourself according to your current status.

4: All of the time; 3: Most of the time; 2: Some of the time; 1: Rarely; 0: Not at all

1. _____ I actively seek opportunities to do tzedakah (opportunities to show kindness and be generous to others)
2. _____ I encourage others to be kind and generous
3. _____ When I see someone in need, I look for ways to meet that need
4. _____ I pray for the needs of others more than I pray for my needs
5. _____ I give away 10% of my income

Add your score for 1-5. Divide by 5.
4- Great job! Keep up the good work of kindness and generosity
3- Good job. Continue to be kind and generous. Seek more opportunities to do tzedakah.
2- You are getting there. Increase your kindness and generosity toward others.
0 or 1- Congratulations. You have identified your need to be more kind and generous toward others. Watch the positive changes that will begin to take place in your life as you improve this area of your life.

Here are a few ideas below of various acts of tzedakah you can engage in over the next 30 days.

30 Days of Tzedakah

1. Tithe (give 10% of your income) to a church or charity which helps people in need.
2. Help someone accomplish a goal.
3. Be an accountability partner for someone working towards a goal.
4. Write or give a thank you note or card to a veteran or person for their service.
5. Write a letter to someone in a nursing home (ask the nursing home to give it to someone that does not have visitors).
6. Give a grocery card to a person or family in need.
7. Pay the grocery bill of the person in front of you in the check-out line.
8. Buy/ cook a meal for someone grieving.
9. Buy/ cook a meal for a single mom who is struggling.
10. Invite an out of state college student to enjoy a holiday meal with you and your family.
11. Adopt an out of state college student.
12. Cut and manicure the lawn (or shovel the snow) of an elderly person.
13. Give a gasoline gift card to a person or family in need.
14. Fix or pay to fix someone's car.
15. Detail your spouse's car. Put a card and their favorite treat on the driver's seat
16. Host a stay warm drive (place a large bin on your lawn for neighbors to donate blankets, coats, hats, gloves, and socks for the homeless). Take donations to a local charity or to an area with homeless people on the streets (and give donations directly to them). Remember to place yard signs around the neighborhood to direct traffic to your bin.
17. Volunteer at a Children's Hospital or local homeless shelter.

18. Visit someone who has been sick or injured
19. Plan an inner city block party with a local church.
20. Refer 3 people to try the product or service of an entrepreneur to help their business.
21. Compliment a cashier/ waiter/ waitress.
22. Visit someone in prison or write them a letter.
23. Volunteer to read for story time at a local library.
24. Take bagels/ fruit/ treats to your child's school for the staff.
25. Pay for a child in need to participate in extra-curricular activities.
26. Take trash bags to clean a block with litter.
27. Write a kind note and place it on someone's windshield.
28. Help a new mom with chores.
29. Take a fatherless boy to the barber's shop, then spend the rest of the afternoon enjoying sports and/ outdoor activities.
30. Take a motherless girl to the hair salon, then spend the rest of the afternoon skating and/ shopping.

50 Scriptures On Tzedakah To Medidtate On During 50 days of Seeking Tzedakah (Righteousness)

Deuteronomy 6:25
Deuteronomy 24:12-13
1Samuel 26:23
Job 33:26
Psalm 11:7
Psalm 23:3
Psalm 103:6
Psalm 111:2-3
Psalm 119:40
Proverbs 11:5
Proverbs 11:18
Proverbs 13:6
Proverbs 15:9
Proverbs 16:12
Proverbs 21:21
Isaiah 5:16
Isaiah 45:8
Isaiah 59:17
Hosea 10:12
Matthew 5:6
John 7-8
Acts 17:31
2Corinthians 9:10
Ephesians 5:9
1John 3:7

Leviticus 19:15
Deuteronomy 15:7-8
2Chronicles 6:23
Psalm 5:8
Psalm 15:1-2
Psalm 71:24
Psalm 106:3
Psalm 112
Proverbs 10:2
Proverbs 11:6
Proverbs 12:28
Proverbs 14:34
Proverbs 16:8
Proverbs 21:3
Isaiah 1:27
Isaiah 32:17
Isaiah 54:14
Isaiah 61:10-11
Amos 5:2
Matthew 6:33
Acts 10:35
Romans 14:17
Ephesians 4:24
1John 2:29
Revelation 19:7-8

About the Author

Anderick Biddle is the Co-Founder and Director of Amazing Kingdom Institute along with his wife Shirron. He has been called by God and appointed as a lead ambassador and educator of the Kingdom of God. His mission is to teach and help train scholars in the knowledge of the Kingdom of God and His righteousness who are equipped to cultivate the culture of the Kingdom within their sphere of influence. They are the parents of Aaron, Josiah, Mikiyah and Shemiyah.

Other books by this author:

THE GOVERNMENT UPON HIS SHOULDER- ORDERING AND ESTABLISHING THE KINGDOM

For additional articles, classes, and resources please visit:
http://kingdomreport.wordpress.com

www.ingramcontent.com/pod-product-compliance
Lightning Source LLC
Chambersburg PA
CBHW032119090426
42743CB00007B/404